Dog's Best Friend

by the same author

Problem Dog: Behaviour and Misbehaviour

VALERIE O'FARRELL

Dog's Best Friend

How Not To Be A Problem Owner

Methuen

First published in Great Britain in 1994
by Methuen London
an imprint of Reed Consumer Books Ltd
Michelin House, 81 Fulham Road, London SW3 6RB
and Auckland, Melbourne, Singapore and Toronto

A CIP catalogue record for this book
is available at the British Library
ISBN 0 413 66000 1

Typeset by Wilmaset Ltd, Birkenhead, Wirral
Printed in Great Britain
by Mackays of Chatham plc

To my father, Nigel Walker, from whom I learnt the pleasure of trying to put ideas into words

Contents

Illustrations

Illustrations acknowledgements

I should like to express my thanks to the following for permission to reproduce copyright material:

The Bibliothèque Nationale, Paris, for an illustration from 'Les Déduits de la Chasse des Bestes Sauvaiges'; the British Library for illustrations from *A Dog's Elegy or Rupert's Tears* (1644) and *The Discovery of Witches* (1647); Detroit Free Press for 'Taken in Raid' by Bob Scott (2 October 1978); Gerald Duckworth and Co. Ltd for an illustration from Judith Neville Lytton's *Toy Dogs* (1911); The Hulton Deutsch Collection Ltd for 'Kate and her dogs'; James Kirkup for his photograph of J. R. Ackerley and Queenie; Jim Macdonald of the SSPCA for his photographs of Tara (*Edinburgh Evening News*, 28 February 1992); *Punch* Picture Library for 'Dog Fashions for 1889' (26 January 1889) and 'It's a little chilly . . .' (2 May 1956); Woodhouse Publishers for a photograph from Barbara Woodhouse's *Dog Training My Way* (1973); and their respective owners for the photographs of Tear-Away and Livingstone.

Text acknowledgements

I should like to express my thanks to the following for permission to use copyright material:

Alan Audley for 'Sultan – A True Story' which first appeared in *The Service Dog*; Professor Christopher Cornford for 'A Child's Dream' by Frances Cornford; *Dog World* for various extracts; David Higham Associates for extracts from *My Dog Tulip* by J. R. Ackerley; the Humane Society of the United States for an extract from their report on dog fighting and Mary Roslin-Williams and *Dog World* for 'A Ghost Story'.

I am grateful to have been able to use material from the following:

Never in Anger by Jean Briggs, the *Daily Telegraph*, *Dogs Today*, *Dog World*, the *Guardian*, *Faithful to the End* by Celia Haddon, LICC Newsletter 1985, *De Canibus* by R. H. A. Merlen, *Training Dogs* by Konrad Most, *The Animal Estate* by Harriet Ritvo, *The Times*, *The Border Terrier* by Anne Roslin-Williams, the *Scotsman*, *The English Dog at Home* by Felicity Wigan, *Dog Training My Way* by Barbara Woodhouse and the *Edinburgh Evening News*.

I should also like to thank the following for their help:

the staff of *Dogs Today* and *Dog World*, Andrew Edney, James Serpell, Nigel Shepley, Mary Stewart, the SSPCA, Shona Watt and all the dog owners who wrote to me or completed my questionnaire.

Introduction

This book is in some ways a sequel to *Problem Dog* (first published in 1989, also by Methuen). As I wrote in the Introduction to that book, I am not a doggy person (although I own dogs) and it is not a doggy book, but a scientific one. I am a psychologist and at the Veterinary School at Edinburgh University I run a clinic for dogs and cats with behaviour problems, where I discuss with the owners the causes of their pets' behaviour and possible ways of changing it. These methods are based on psychological principles: the aim of *Problem Dog* was to make these principles directly accessible to owners so that they could carry out their own diagnosis and treatment.

When I told people I met what I did at the Veterinary School they often used to laugh or else remark, 'Of course it's the fault of the owners, isn't it?' But the recent public discussion surrounding the passing of the Dangerous Dogs Act (1991) has at least reduced the frequency of these irritating reactions. Most people now realise that at least some problem dogs are no joke. They also realise that some dogs, such as pit bulls, are genetically endowed with a temperament which is liable to make them a problem to most owners. On the other hand, there are some owners who are so uncaring or so deranged that they would make most dogs into a problem. But both kinds of extreme are rare. Most behaviour problems in dogs, like most marital problems, are the result of mismatches or misunderstandings to which both members of the couple make a contribution.

But there is no doubt that many owners have strong feelings about their dogs and that their dogs can play important parts in their lives. Some pet dogs are just as much working dogs as any farm collie, except that the work that they do is emotional rather than physical. And it is not only dog lovers who have strong feelings about dogs: there are passionate dog haters and dog fearers. As a clinical psychologist most of whose work is with the psychological problems of individual human patients and human couples, I find fascinating the complexity and variety of these interactions between dogs and people.

When discussing their feelings about their dogs, people may make intimate personal revelations. Publishing what they tell me can create an ethical problem of confidentiality. As I explain in Chapter 2, some owners wrote to me (or completed a questionnaire) knowing that they were providing potential material for a book. I am very grateful to them for taking this trouble (especially when this clearly caused them emotional pain) and I have taken the context in which they wrote as permission to reproduce it. Where it seemed advisable, I have preserved the writer's anonymity by altering inessential details. I have altered accounts of problem dogs I have treated in the same way. From certain human patients who have been in psychotherapy with me I have learnt a great deal about the richness and complexity of the meaning of a dog to his owner. None of this material appears in the book: I would not invite someone inside my mind and confide my most intimate thoughts to her if I knew they might appear in a book, even in a disguised form.

My previous book, *Problem Dog*, explored the mind of the dog. The purpose of this book is to explore attitudes towards dogs, both of the individual and of society. I hope that, as well as finding this interesting for its own sake, readers will be able to use the exploration to improve their own relationships with their dogs.

Part I
What Dogs Do to People

1 ● *On becoming a Dog Owner*

Dogs arouse strong and complicated feelings in people. Lifelong dog owners take this fact for granted, but I entered the dog world for the first time in my thirties and I was quite unprepared for it. I had always wanted a dog. (Actually, I wanted a monkey, but I had to give up that fantasy early on in life.) But it was only when I was married and settled with a house, garden and children that it became feasible.

The kitchen had a large cat-flap and, when I considered what breed of dog to get, it seemed a neat idea to get one which could go through the cat-flap: it would save a lot of trouble. The hole looked sort of dachshund-shaped to me, but when I discussed the matter with a family friend, she had a better idea. Dachshunds were not suitable for children, she said. A dog like hers, a Cavalier King Charles spaniel, would be better.

I mentioned my dog-owning intentions to the headmistress of my daughter's nursery school. She was an intimidating woman, with a bun and fixed theoretical views on child-rearing and child development. She made it clear that she considered that the mothers of her children were woefully incompetent and that the children survived only because of their daily dose of nursery school. I knew she was a dog lover because she sometimes brought one of her Alsatians into work. I once came across a mother in tears on the pavement. She had been in the school, collecting her child, when the dog had suddenly bounded out of the office. She was startled: the child was terrified. The headmistress was censorious: she told the mother that it was a sign of 'serious disturbance' to be afraid of dogs. This woman loomed large in the lives of us mothers at the time and perhaps I thought that chit-chat about dogs would ingratiate me with her. If I did, I was mistaken. She was horrified that I should even contemplate getting a dog. She implied that I might just about be capable of looking after a child, but looking after a dog was quite beyond me.

Fortunately, I was not quite enough in awe of her to be deterred. I answered an advertisement in the newspaper for Cavalier puppies. The ones in that litter were all spoken for, but the breeder, Mrs C, invited us over to see them anyway. While we cooed over the puppies, she questioned me in minute detail about my domestic circumstances. Although she expressed herself more tactfully, Mrs C obviously felt, like the headmistress, that only certain people were qualified to keep dogs. But this time, I passed muster. (In fact, eventually we became close friends.) About a fortnight later, she rang me to say that one of her friends, a 'top breeder in Scotland', had a litter of ten-week-old puppies. It was February of the very severe winter of 1979. This breeder lived in the Highlands and had been snowed up for the past couple of months: no one had been able to come to see her litter. I was very lucky to have the chance of such a good puppy.

The roads were by then just passable, so I set off next morning from Edinburgh with my four- and two-year-old daughters in our old Renault. When we eventually found the 'top breeder's' but-and-ben somewhere off the A9, all three of us were feeling a bit fractious. The top breeder looked rather like the nursery headmistress and – by the look on her face when she saw us – shared her views on my suitability as a dog owner. Her doubts clearly increased when she opened the kitchen door and released a beige-coloured flood of Labradors. The two-year-old screamed and jumped into my arms. The top breeder made a tutting noise: clearly this fear was a sign of serious disturbance. I, too, was disconcerted. It had not occurred to me that my children might feel like the boy at the nursery. A picture of a totally unmanageable domestic situation, with both children terrified of the puppy, flashed through my mind. But it was too late to get out of it now.

The top breeder, whatever her reservations, obviously felt that too. We went on through the kitchen and on out of the back door to a kind of hen house and run (still covered in snow) where the puppies were kept. The puppy was duly chosen – the top breeder sensibly recommended that we not take the puppy which rushed up to the four-year-old and knocked her over, much to her delight (the two-year-old still hovered nervously in the background), but take the less exuberantly friendly one. We picked our way back over the snowy ground to the kitchen. The top breeder opened a tin. Perhaps, I thought hopefully, there might be a cup of tea. It had been a long journey there and it would be a long journey back. A digestive biscuit was indeed produced, but it turned out to be for the puppy. The top breeder tenderly wrapped her in an old woolly jumper, kissed her goodbye, shot us a final censorious look and gave her the biscuit as a parting present.

Back in Edinburgh, we settled into our new status as dog owners. We all fell in love with the puppy, Mhairi, even the two-year-old. She went everywhere with us. It seemed easiest, when shopping locally, to push her and the two-year-old around in a pram. She became a favourite with the shopkeepers: some would run out from behind their counters with sweeties for her. Things were different in the centre of Edinburgh. I was once ordered out of Marks and Spencer, who do not allow dogs. I was shocked, because by then Mhairi seemed to me more like a baby than a dog. I refused to leave, arguing that, since she was in a pram, she was not in contact with any part of the shop and that they therefore had no right to object to her. The supervisor – who by that time had been summoned – gave me a funny look and left me alone.

Not surprisingly, under this regime, Mhairi grew up thinking she was a human being. In spite of her weeks in the hen run with the other puppies, she was not much interested in other dogs. But she was very interested in people. Once out of her pram and on a lead, she would rush enthusiastically up to people in shops. The shopkeepers still greeted her as a friend and gave her sweeties. The response of customers, total strangers, was more unpredictable. As a fond parent, I had no empathy with those who recoiled from the dirty paws and the snuffling nose. But I remember one reaction which was quite different from run-of-the-mill disapproval. In the chemist's, Mhairi ran up to a middle-aged man in a tweed jacket. He turned round and with a bellow of rage struck her with his stick so that she yelped and jumped backwards into a display cabinet. 'Bloody dogs, they should be exterminated!' he shouted and rushed out of the shop. This incident did not prompt me to wonder whether it was inconsiderate to allow my dog such free access to the public, but, as a doting dog-parent, led me to marvel at the twisted minds of some people.

To lifelong dog owners, the reactions of these people – dog lovers, dog haters, dog fearers – will not be at all surprising. But, at the time, they came as a surprise to me. When, six years earlier, we had acquired a kitten – two kittens in fact – no one had seen fit to judge whether we were suitable owners or not, least of all the people we got them from. They were only too glad to find homes for them and had given us a glass of sherry when we picked them up. I did not push the kittens around in a pram. No one had shown hatred or fear of them, unless you count one friend who couldn't visit us because of an allergy.

Since I have been working in the field of dog behaviour, I have been even more impressed by the interesting and peculiar part which dogs play in our lives. I have come across owners who have contemplated suicide if their dogs were destroyed (see Chapter 9); an owner who thought her dog could work the washing machine (Chapter 3); pensioners who spend half their pension on feeding their dogs (Chapter 3). I have also come across people who feed dogs poisoned meat (Chapter 9) or keep them in cupboards (Chapter 11).

This polarisation of attitudes has a public face, too. There are societies dedicated to the defence and protection of dogs. There are papers for dog breeders and, a more recent development, magazines for the ordinary dog lover. These carry features such as dog obituaries, 'Angel in Disguise – a Rottweiler Story with a Difference!', 'Shaggy Dog Tails by Mungo' ('sociable dogs can holiday with Mungo at the Featherbed Country Club for Dogs, just telephone . . . and ask his Missus for details') and advertisements for 'Kaynine sanitary belts. Fully washable and in 6 sizes'.

On the other side of the barricades is LICC (League for the Introduction of Canine Controls) which was formed as a result of the support received by Polly Toynbee for her article in the *Guardian*, January 1978. In this article Ms Toynbee says she reads 'with glee the stories of the Chinese rounding up dogs and herding them into electrified fences'. She ends with a 'modest proposal' for dealing with the dog problem. 'Let dogs eat dog meat, thus rapidly reducing the dog population. Eventually there would be just one dog left which could be put in a zoo.'

Printed posters are sometimes displayed, presumably produced (though not claimed) by some organisation, with slogans such as 'Crucify a dog for Easter'.

As well as the more extreme pro- or anti-dog attitudes, there are those whose behaviour is a puzzling mixture of contradictions.

Mr M took the trouble to consult me about his Pekingese, Ming, who growled and snapped when he was groomed. It was clear that Ming was a dominant dog and I explained to Mr M how to reduce that dominance. Because I sensed that Mr M was feeling rather desperate and needed the situation to be resolved quickly, I suggested that a short course of Ovarid (a synthetic female hormone) might help to make Ming more amenable. Mr M turned down the idea out of hand, not because the drug might have harmful side-effects, but because he felt it would make Ming less male. I also recommended that until Mr M had established his dominance over Ming, he should refrain from grooming him and so provoking the aggression. Mr M said that this was impossible as Ming had to be groomed every day. I suggested that if Ming's coat were cut short, as a temporary measure, this might help. Mr M was horrified at the very idea. A few days later Mr M apparently took Ming to his vet to have him destroyed, because he had bitten him again.

Accounts appear regularly in the dog press of well-known breeders or dog rescuers who neglect or ill-treat their dogs (see Chapter 11). I believe that these cases of contradictory behaviour are extreme examples of what most dog owners do. Some owners may love and care for their dogs unfailingly. But most of us, I suspect, cuddle them and are sentimental about them sometimes and at other times forget them or shout at them for things which aren't their fault. These intense and contradictory emotions are intriguing in themselves and one of the purposes of this book is to explore the deeper reasons for them. But they also have practical implications. Responding to these feelings without insight can lead to problems. In 1991, the Dangerous Dogs Act was passed, imposing conditions on the ownership of certain breeds – in practice, mostly pit bull terriers (see Chapter 9). The bill was the Government's response to public emotion about dog attacks. This emotion had been building up for a year or two, but the immediate trigger was a serious attack on a little girl by a pit bull. Because it was prompted by emotion rather than reason, the Bill was rushed through hastily and its provisions were muddled. For example, there is no objective way of distinguishing between a pit bull terrier and the much more common Staffordshire bull terrier, which it closely resembles. This has led to impasses such as the case of Bosun, reported in the *Daily Telegraph*, July 1992:

> *Owned by an East London family and still in kennels after being seized by police in January. Bosun's case has been to court seven times. Two Staffordshire bull terrier judges have sworn that Bosun is not a pit bull terrier but is a cross-bred Stafford but . . . a RSPCA officer and a veterinary surgeon said the dog was a pit bull.*

Also, although there is no doubt that pit bulls are more dangerous than the average dog, it is unlikely that this provision of the Act will significantly reduce the number of dog attacks, most of which are carried out by other breeds of dog (see Chapter 9).

At an individual level, too, intense emotions about dogs can cause problems. The number of dogs which are destroyed for behavioural reasons, abandoned, passed on to other owners or left in animals shelters, bears witness to the failure of dog/owner relationships. If the owners who consult me about problem behaviour in their dogs are anything to go by, most of the dogs themselves make a contribution to this failure: they have inherited either nervous or aggressive temperaments; they may also have been psychologically damaged as young puppies, usually by an impoverished environment. In most cases, the owners too are partly responsible, either because they misunderstand the dog's behaviour or because they have unrealistic expectations of him. Sometimes these misunderstandings and false expectations are due purely to ignorance, but more often they are due partly to the owner's psychological needs and conflicts. Some animal behaviourists, for example Dr Roger Mugford, disagree violently with this idea. They argue that the majority of their clients are normal, decent people. But this is to miss the point. All of us have needs and conflicts: for example, it is clear to me, looking back, that Mhairi as a puppy in her pram was to me a substitute third baby. The animal rights movement is correct when it maintains that pet dogs are exploited to satisfy these needs. But usually this exploitation does not matter. Most owners and dogs have happy relationships either because the dog is adaptable or because the personality of dog and owner fit together. (In spite of her babyfication, Mhairi grew up to be a normal and problem-free dog.) But the chance of a happy relationship can be increased even more if the owner has some insight into his own needs. He can then pick a dog who is likely to satisfy them. Or, if it is too late for that, he can take precautions to protect the dog from the adverse effects of those needs.

2 ● *Dogs and Human Emotions*

Why do dogs arouse such powerful and irrational emotions in us? Our feelings of love and hatred, normally reserved for human beings, are also directed at dogs. They are cast in this role more often than other pets because we can have with them a relationship which is more similar to the relationship we can have with a person. Dogs are by nature pack animals and instinctively want to form relationships with other pack members. A dog who has mixed with people as a puppy will regard them as honorary dogs and will relate to them as he would to other dogs. He uses an instinctive repertoire of body language to communicate with these other pack members, which include his human family. What is more, this body language is similar enough to ours for us to be able to understand most of it immediately and instinctively. If your dog bounds up to you and tries to lick your face, it is hard to miss the message that he is pleased to see you. If you try to take his bone away and he growls, that message is pretty clear too. And, of course, the communication goes in the other direction too: dogs respond with excitement to an excited tone of voice, they look guilty when we speak to them crossly.

This ability to communicate puts the dog in a different league from other pets, such as fish. Every so often in a pet-fish-keeping magazine there appears a rather touching letter from a reader whose fish 'recognises' him. These fish are usually of the cichlid family (which includes angel fish, discus etc.) who have (as fish go) highly developed social behaviour patterns: a male and a female form a lasting pair bond and they protect their eggs and newly hatched fry, either by chasing away predators, or, in the case of some species, by taking them into their mouths. But even fish as sophisticated as this are incapable of interacting socially with people. The difference in body size and structure and in the vocabulary of the body language is too great. If a fish becomes excited when its owner appears, this is because it has learned to associate what is, to it, a meaningless thing, the human form, with something which is highly meaningful, such as food or a water change.

The same applies to small rodents such as hamsters. If they are handled often enough and from an early age, they will become tame. They will allow themselves to be picked up and they will run up and down your arm and not bite you. But when they are doing this, they are just treating you as a piece of the furniture: there is no social interaction involved.

Budgies are different: if, like dogs, they see enough of people early on in life, they become imprinted on human beings and they treat them like honorary budgies. Konrad Lorenz, the German ethologist, was the first scientist seriously to investigate this early learning phenomenon: in *King Solomon's Ring* he tells a story about a pet jackdaw whom he reared apart from other jackdaws. It became very attached to him and would court him and try to feed him worms via his ear. Owners who buy single budgies as eight-week-old chicks can end up in a situation similar to Lorenz with budgies who are interested exclusively in them. As with dogs, real social interaction goes on. Budgies and owners talk to each other (irrespective of whether or not the owner has taught it recognisable English words): the essence of the communication is that one of them makes a noise and the other replies with a noise. Budgies make sexual advances to their owners by running up and down the perch and bowing. They also groom them (this can be rather tickly, even painful). They may also offer their owners food. An owner attached enough to his budgie to make the effort can usually understand these social signals. But they do not have the same direct appeal as a dog's behaviour, because they are so different from our own social signals: communicating with a budgie is a bit like learning to talk to a man from Mars.

Cats are different again. Like dogs and budgies they have an instinctive body language for communicating with members of the same species and, if they mix with people as kittens, they regard them thereafter as honorary cats. Their body language is easier to understand than a budgie's: sitting on your knee or twining round your legs obviously shows affection; going behind the sofa or growling and spitting equals dislike. But, unlike dogs, adult cats in the wild state are not necessarily social beings. Some feral cats lead solitary lives. They may have territories which partly overlap the territories of other cats, but they take care to time their movements so as to avoid coming face to face with those other cats. But they are capable of living sociably with other cats if they have to: for example, if someone becomes concerned about the welfare of feral cats in a neighbourhood and regularly sets out food for them, they will congregate around the feeding place and form a social group. Normally this consists of a stable group of females (usually mother and daughters) with males more loosely attached. In the same way, a cat's social life with his owner is often an optional, on/off affair: sometimes they feel sociable and sometimes they don't. Most dogs are always sociable because their instinct tells them that their lives depend on it. For a dog's wild ancestor, the wolf, the pack is essential. Without it, wolves could not catch large prey, such as deer. A female wolf with cubs also relies on her fellow pack members to help with the care of the cubs and also in the first few weeks of the cubs' life, when she hardly leaves them, to bring her food. So a wolf's life depends on his relationship with his pack members and dogs have inherited those instincts.

People who prefer cats to dogs often find the dog's dependence on human company a strain, like a visitor who expects constant entertainment. They feel easier with the semi-self-reliance of the cat. They may also find attractive the cat's characteristic of sometimes wanting you and sometimes not; like pursuing a human sexual partner who is playing hard to get.

This is not the whole story. Owners may relate to their dogs as if they were people, but most owners are quite clear about the distinction. When, very rarely, one comes across someone who talks or behaves otherwise, the effect can be disturbing. For example, in Chapter 3 I describe a conversation with an owner who talked quite seriously about her dog bursting into tears. It was hard to know what to say to her. Also, in Chapter 7 I discuss people who love their dogs passionately, more than anyone else in the world. Some of these accounts are unsettling. (It is possible that, in the past, this unsettling effect may have led such people to be branded as witches. One sign of being a witch was having a 'familiar', a close animal companion.)

Also, there are differences in the ways we show our emotions towards dogs and towards people. For example, it is socially acceptable to behave in an emotionally intimate way with a perfectly strange dog.

> On one occasion, when Mhairi was grown up, a man called to read the electricity meter. As I let him in, he started to grumble that he had called before and not found anyone in. I asked him why he had not estimated the reading as usual? As we stood bickering in the hall, Mhairi trotted out of the kitchen and, as was her wont with strange men, rushed to greet him. Without a pause, he switched from talking in stiff, official tones about 'right of access' to murmuring tender endearments. 'My bonny lass,' he cooed as he scratched behind Mhairi's ears, 'my braw wee bairn.' Then, without any sense of incongruity, he turned back to me and continued with his lecture about the responsibilities of owning an electricity meter.

In the same way, emotions about our own dogs are liable to burst out with disconcerting suddenness.

> In a television programme on pet cremation, a curious sequence appeared which had nothing to do with cremation: it was probably there because it had the same disturbing effect on the producer that it had on me. A woman and her husband had brought an elderly wire-haired terrier of some kind to their vet for euthanasia. We saw her explaining to the vet in a rational, matter-of-fact tone why this was the right thing: Rags was messing all the time in the house, he was also blind and he wouldn't get any better, would he? The vet agreed in a non-committal way (perhaps the presence of the cameras made them all self-conscious) and proceeded to give the fatal injection. The couple looked on impassively, but when the vet finally announced that Rags was dead, the woman suddenly threw herself into a frenzy of grief: swaying about, she wailed, 'Oh Rags, Rags, Rags, what have I done!' This went on for about thirty seconds, with husband and vet looking on silently: they seemed embarrassed and at a loss. Then the outburst finished as suddenly as it had begun. 'Thank you very much,' she said, 'what do we owe you?'

Then there is the 'cringe' factor. It is difficult for an owner to talk (or write) about his feelings for his dog without running the risk of being sentimental or embarrassing. But what makes one listener cringe, another may find deeply moving. A genre which I personally find hard to stomach is an account of a dog's life written from the dog's point of view: for example, 'Shaggy Dog Tails by Mungo' in Chapter 1. Also I once felt impelled to leave a talk on cruelty to dogs and take a brisk walk round the block, not because I could not bear to hear about the acts of cruelty described, but, for some reason, I could not stand the fact that the speaker was almost in tears. On the other hand, I am never embarrassed by the things which clients tell me about themselves and their dogs, nor by any of the owners' replies to my questionnaire (see below).

Many owners are aware that others find their feelings for their dogs embarrassing or funny. (Humour is one way of coping with embarrassment.) They are usually circumspect about whom they confide in and may feel slightly ashamed of their own feelings.

> An illustration of this was a news item I heard on the radio just after the Falklands war. It featured an army chaplain talking to troops who had just been fighting there. He said that probably most of them, when under fire or just before going into combat, had thought about the person who meant most to them. He urged them not to forget the intensity of the feeling they had at that moment or the conviction that this was the most important thing in life. 'Whether,' he said, 'that relationship is with your wife, your girlfriend, your parents' – his audience listened to this in silence – 'or with your dog' – and here his audience, as he had intended, burst out laughing.

Organisations which are pro-dogs (or pro-pets in general) by and large try to ignore the joke/cringe factor. I suppose they feel it undermines the seriousness of their purpose. But this factor is an important clue to the nature of the difference between a relationship with a dog and a relationship with a person. It needs to be explained; to ignore it is to distort the whole field of study.

I don't think there is a single, simple explanation for the phenomena I have just described. I suggest that one reason is that our interactions with people are both rational and emotional. As well as loving and getting angry with the adult human members of our family, we cooperate with them in running our affairs. This involves rational discussions about, for example, how to pay the mortgage or where to go on holiday. With a dog, none of this rational discussion is possible. We relate to him on the basis of pure emotion. Our relationship with our dog is similar to the very first relationship we have in our lives: with our mothers. Babies don't discuss the mortgage with their mothers or even how to make up a feed: they just feel angry, hungry or happy as the case may be. Most dogs are the same. Their naked emotionality means that they tap into a primitive level of emotion in their owners: the kind of emotion their owners experienced as babies.

This effect is enhanced by the fact that the things dogs do and the emotions they express embody precisely those issues which are central for all of us from babyhood onwards. Most of the time we try to ignore these big issues because they are so painful; or at least we try to conceal our emotions from other people because they make us so vulnerable. But a dog has no such inhibitions: he does not hide what he feels or try to keep a stiff upper lip. He jumps all over you when he is pleased to see you and barks or growls when he is annoyed. There are three main kinds of emotion or activity which dogs are good at expressing. They will be discussed in more detail in later chapters but briefly they are:

1. Love and attachment. A dog who is attached to you makes no secret of the fact: he runs up to greet you when you get home and may even follow you from room to room. And a dog who is upset by your going out doesn't try to pretend that he doesn't mind or distract himself by keeping busy. He follows you to the door looking upset, he may bark or howl as you walk down the path and he may scrabble at the door in an attempt to follow you.

2. Hate and aggression. One reason why dogs have become domesticated is that their aggression is comparatively easily to control. But when they do express it, it is often in a dramatic and unmistakable way: growling, snarling or biting. From babyhood, one of our most difficult emotional tasks is coping with the anger we feel towards those we love. Anger and hate are emotions we often try to ignore in ourselves and being confronted with something nakedly ferocious is often very disturbing (Chapter 9).

3. Messiness. Dogs chew things up, they smell, they

leave hairs on clothes and furniture. As will be discussed in Chapter 10, coping with the messy bits in ourselves is another important human problem. It starts with potty training or even earlier and continues throughout life, in less concrete more metaphorical ways.

Because dogs by their behaviour bring these issues to the fore in a childlike way, our response to them tends to be correspondingly childlike. This is why, in contrast to most of our day-to-day 'civilised' behaviour towards the human adults around us, our behaviour towards dogs tends to be irrational, emotional and inconsistent. It is partly our awareness of the childishness of these emotions which makes us sometimes embarrassed about them and sometimes makes them embarrassing to others.

There is another factor at work too. Each of us sees reality from a slightly different perspective. To our dealings with those around us we bring our own assumptions and wishes. One person may crave approval, another may expect people to do him down, yet another may feel superior and contemptuous towards those around him. This is to over-simplify matters because we each of us have a complex system of needs, assumptions and fears, some of which are contradictory. For example, we have feelings of both anger and love towards those nearest to us. Most of the time we do not allow ourselves to be consciously aware of these contradictions, because they make us feel so uncomfortable. Nevertheless, unconsciously, a great deal of our emotional energy is taken up with trying to deal with them. And, as I hope to show in the rest of this book, dogs help us to live with these conflicts. They do this because, to use a psychoanalytic term, we 'project' problematic emotions onto dogs, where they are easier to deal with. For example, as we shall see in Chapter 3, an owner may deal with a painful need in herself to be loved and looked after by loving and looking after a dog. Or, as described in Chapter 9, aggression towards others may be expressed through a snappy dog.

A useful way of thinking of this emotional luggage of unconscious needs and conflicts which each of us carries is to suppose that each of us has, going on inside us, an internal drama or scenario, which both poses problems and offers solutions. All through our lives, we try to play out these internal dramas, using the people around us. But the basic themes of the scenarios are determined very early in life:

> Miss S had a mother who was basically loving and caring but who could not bear Miss S being very upset. As a baby, there were times when Miss S (like most babies) would cry and cry for no obvious reason. When this happened, her mother would put her back in her cot, go away and leave her until she stopped. As a toddler, Miss S sometimes became inconsolably upset: for example, when her father stopped playing with her and left for work. Again her mother could not bear her crying and would lock herself in the bathroom. Miss S grew up with an internal scenario of a crying, needy baby and a deserting mother. As an adult, she played out this scenario in her relationships with men. She was attractive and readily entered into relationships on a superficial level, but always kept something of herself back. She only became involved with men who needed her more than she needed them: they played the part of the crying baby and she played the part of the deserting mother.

Although other human beings are the obvious candidates to play parts in these scenarios, dogs can play parts as well; in fact, in many ways, they are better at it than people. For one thing, as we have seen, they express vividly and openly the kinds of primitive emotion which are involved in these internal dramas. For example, a dog would have made an excellent baby for Miss S's scenario.

It is also easier to find a dog suitable for your own particular scenario than it is to find a person. If you want to find a clinging, dependent woman to marry (even if you are not consciously aware of it yourself) you have to meet a lot of women and get to know them before you can find out whether they would suit you. With a dog, it is easier to buy one 'off the peg' to suit your needs. Different breeds have different typical temperaments and one advantage of pedigree dogs is that their personalities can be predicted to some extent. Certainly, there are timid Rottweilers and vicious Cavalier King Charles spaniels. But there is less variation than in the personalities of mongrels or cross-breeds. Also, most dogs are so keen to please their owners that they learn to fit in even better with their owners' scenarios. For example, a dog can learn to be even more aggressive and protective than he is by instinct; or to be even more dependent and clinging.

Freud said that dreams were 'a royal road to the unconscious'; in other words, that they reveal a great deal about the dreamer's internal scenario. The same could be said of an owner's relationship with his dog. This is yet another reason for the cringe factor. Owners may feel embarrassed about their attachment to their dogs, because they realise, perhaps without being fully aware of it, that this attachment reveals more about them than they would wish. And listeners may feel embarrassed for the same reason: they know that they are hearing more than the speaker wants to tell them.

Does it matter that we use dogs in this way, to help us in our emotional life? Here we must distinguish between successful and unsuccessful scenarios. In a successful scenario, the dog is able to play the part allotted to him without too much strain; dog and owner live happily together, enjoying each other's company. In an unsuccessful scenario, the dog is unable to play the part expected of him: the quality of the dog's or the owner's life may be impaired; or the owner may get rid of the dog. In most dog/owner relationships, the scenario is neither completely successful nor completely unsuccessful, but somewhere in between. The rest of this book will look at various ways in which scenarios can fail, but broadly speaking there are two reasons. The dog may be mis-cast: for example, if the owner wants someone to boss about, but the dog is excitable and more interested in chasing squirrels. Or the part may be impossible for any dog to play: he may be expected to guard the house, but to be friendly towards the postman.

At an individual level, being aware of the parts dogs play in your own scenarios can help you to have a more satisfactory relationship with them. You can maximise the chances of picking a dog who will fit happily into your scenario. You can modify your expectations of your dog so that he is more likely to be able to fit into it. And you can change your behaviour towards him in ways which can extricate you from a damned scenario.

Dogs can take part in other internal dramas besides those of their owners. They can loom large in the mental life of dog phobics and dog haters. They also seem to play a part in national scenarios as reflected in the media. There are some successful scenarios, which both make people feel good and benefit the dog: the terriers stuck down drainpipes who are rescued by firemen, for example. Unfortunately, society involves dogs in impossible scenarios too. Using this perspective, extreme dog haters and dog lovers in society can be seen as linked. Extreme dog lovers put forward scenarios in which dogs play unrealistically angelic parts: they comfort the old, visit the sick (Pat-dogs), help the disabled (guide dogs for the blind and deaf). If they attack anyone, it is never their fault, but the fault of a feckless owner or silly victim. In the extreme dog hater's scenario, dogs are dangerous beasts, carrying ghastly diseases: in this scenario they are to be banned from public parks, muzzled, castrated and even destroyed. But each side needs the other. Without dog haters, dog lovers would have to come to terms with the unpalatable, non-angelic side of dogs (see Chapters 9 and 10). Without dog lovers, dog haters would sweep the board, get rid of dogs completely and deprive themselves of a satisfactory object of hatred.

The rest of the book examines different kinds of scenario in more detail. Before you embark on it you may like to try out for yourself the tests for owners. When I was planning this book, I realised that I needed to know in detail about the scenarios of lots of ordinary owners, not just the clients who consult me about their problem dogs, so I first of all drew up a questionnaire which asked the kind of nosey personal questions you would not normally dare ask people to their faces. I handed out copies at conferences, I set them out in the waiting room of the Small Animal Clinic at the Edinburgh Veterinary School: I also persuaded a dog paper and a dog magazine to feature it. I should like to thank all those who took the trouble to fill it in, especially those who did so in great detail and at the cost of digging up painful memories. I can assure them that if I have used their story in this book I have taken great care to alter circumstantial details, so that, although they may recognise themselves, their friends will not. Before going any further, other readers who are interested in finding out about their own personal scenarios might like to answer the questionnaire. Even if it is for your own eyes only, I recommend that you write down the answers. Give as much detail as you can.

Questionnaire

1. Which dog in your life have you felt closest to (or your favourite dog)?
2. Describe his/her personality.
3. Why do/did you feel close to him/her?
4. Which dog in your life have you felt least close to (or your least favourite dog)?
5. Describe his/her personality.
6. Why do/did you not feel close to him/her?
7. Describe your father's personality.

8. Describe your relationship with him.
9. Describe your mother's personality.
10. Describe your relationship with her.
11. What has been the main turning point (or crisis) in your life and how did you deal with it?
12. Can you remember dreaming about any of your dogs? If so, describe the dream.

Although I was mainly interested in finding connections and meaning within each individual questionnaire, it also struck me that, comparing a number of these questionnaires with one another, I could test out one of the assumptions on which this book is based: that the part a dog is called upon to play in an owner's scenario is determined by the owner's early relationships, especially his relationships with his parents. Using seventy of the subjects who replied to the questionnaire in enough detail, I looked at the descriptions of their favourite dog. I also looked at their descriptions of their relationships with each of their parents. I classified the decriptions of their favourite dog into those which were idealised and those which were realistic. Idealised descriptions featured only favourable characteristics (e.g. 'faithful and loving' or 'my own special man'). Realistic descriptions included some qualifying comment such as 'greedy' or 'cheeky'. I found that significantly more idealising owners described their relationship with the parent of the same sex as the favourite dog as bad or non-existent; significantly more realistic owners described their relationship with that parent as good or adequate. In other words, the idealising owners were using their dogs to play the part of the good parent whom they had lacked in real life.

When I read the replies to a questionnaire I tried to work out the personal scenario underlying it. In many cases it was not possible to make it out because of lack of information. Sometimes there were intriguing hints but the whole picture didn't quite make sense. There were pieces of the jigsaw missing. In these cases, I often wrote to the owners and asked for more information. If any of these people think they spot themselves as examples in the book, they should not think that this is because they were more crazy than the others. In fact, the opposite is true. They were relaxed enough about their own feelings to express them: my grateful thanks to all of them.

Plotting your own personal scenario

When you look at your own replies to the questionnaire, you may well be unable to make out the scenario underlying it. It is unlikely that you can be detached enough; also you probably have a vested interest in concealing some aspects of it from yourself. If you are interested in looking into it further, you might like to try a method which some psychologists use to explore personal scenarios: the Kelly grid. I tried it out on some of the owners who replied to the questionnaire: some of their grids appear later in the book. The instructions are rather complicated, but I hope that at least people who have done O level or GCSE maths will be able to follow it.

To do this test you will need paper (preferably squared) and pencil. The method is as follows:
1. Start with the form in Figure 1a. (Figure 1b shows a completed form.) Copy this form, preferably onto squared paper.
2. Look at your questionnaire descriptions of dogs and parents. Pick out twelve adjectives which describe personality (e.g. nervous, kind) rather than physical attributes (e.g. tall, old). Use adjectives which could apply either to dogs or people: 'keen on computers' or 'liable to bite' would not do – 'clever' or 'bad-tempered' would be all right. Do not use two adjectives which mean exactly the same thing or exactly the opposite. Fill in these adjectives in boxes a–l.

Figure 1a

	self	mother	father	sister	brother	child	favourite dog	least favourite dog	ideal self	partner	friend	pet	another dog	admired person	helpful person	dog lover	person not trusted	irritating person	pitied person	non dog lover
	1	2	3	4	5	6	7	8	9	10	11	12	13	14	15	16	17	18	19	20
a.																				
b.																				
c.																				
d.																				
e.																				
f.																				
g.																				
h.																				
i.																				
j.																				
k.																				
l.																				

Dimension 1 score

Dimension 2 score

Figure 1b

	self	mother	father	sister	brother	child	favourite dog	least favourite dog	ideal self	partner	friend	pet	another dog	admired person	helpful person	dog lover	person not trusted	irritating person	pitied person	non dog lover
	1	2	3	4	5	6	7	8	9	10	11	12	13	14	15	16	17	18	19	20
a. Happy	X	X		X	X		X		X	X	X	X				X				
b. Autistic				X	X		X				X		X			X	X	X	X	X
c. Confident			X		X				X	X	X	X	X	X	X		X			
d. Unpredictable			X	X	X		X		X				X				X	X		X
e. Well adjusted		X		X		X		X		X	X	X	X	X	X					
f. Quick-tempered	X		X		X	X		X		X			X	X			X			X
g. Willing to please	X	X		X			X		X		X	X			X			X	X	
h. Selfish	X		X	X	X	X		X		X			X			X				X
i. Loving		X		X		X	X		X	X	X	X	X	X						
j. A worrier	X	X		X		X	X	X		X			X					X	X	
k. Understanding		X		X	X		X		X		X			X	X			X	X	
l. Hard-working		X	X		X	X		X		X	X			X	X	X		X		
Dimension 1 score	3	0	5	3	4	5	0	5	0	5	0	0	1	4	2	0	5	2	1	5
Dimension 2 score	0	0	2	0	2	0	0	0	0	2	1	2	2	1	2	2	1	2	0	0	1

3. Next you need a list of names of twenty people or animals you know or have known (except for 1 and 9, which are concerned with yourself). They should fill the following descriptions or categories (if you can't think of a person or animal to fill a particular category, just use any person or animal; the important thing is to have twenty individuals):

1. Yourself
2. Your mother
3. Your father
4. A sister (or someone who is, or was, like a sister to you)
5. A brother (or someone who is, or was, like a brother to you)
6. One of your children (or someone who is, or was, like a child to you)
7. Favourite dog
8. Least favourite dog
9. Yourself as you would like to be
10. Your partner or spouse
11. A friend
12. A pet of another species (e.g. cat)
13. Another dog
14. Someone you admire
15. Someone who has been helpful to you
16. Someone fond of dogs
17. Someone you feel you cannot trust
18. Someone who irritates you
19. Someone you feel sorry for
20. Someone not fond of dogs

On your copy of Figure 1a, fill the names of these people in boxes 1–20, along the top row.

4. Start with adjective a. Pick the ten individuals to which it most applies. Mark them with a cross. For instance, in the completed example (Figure 1b), for her first adjective 'happy' the subject has chosen as her ten happiest individuals: self, mother, sister, brother, favourite dog, ideal self,

partner, friend, pet and dog lover. The others (father, child etc.) are her ten least happy people. Do the same for each of the twelve adjectives.

Scoring

1. The first step is to calculate, for each adjective (a–l), its 'matching score' with each other adjective. These should be filled in in Figure 2a. Starting with the pair of adjectives a and b ('happy' and 'autistic' in the example) count the number of columns which contain either two crosses or two blanks. Thus, in the example, the matching score for a and b is 6 and this is filled in in Figure 2b twice: in row a, column b and row b, column a. Now do the same for rows a and c, rows a and d and so on. You will probably find that the quickest way to do this is to copy the pattern of crosses and blanks for one row (row a in this case) onto the edge of another sheet of paper and move that copy systematically down the other rows, placing it under each row in turn. When you have done this for all the rows, you should end up with a completed Figure 2a which looks something like Figure 2b (see page 30).

2. Each matching score in Figures 2a and 2b is a form of correlation: a measure of the degree to which, in your mind, each of the twelve adjectives is associated with each of the others. For instance, in the example, the matching score for adjectives f 'quick-tempered' and h 'selfish' is 18. The highest possible score is 20. A score of 18 therefore indicates a close association: for this subject, most people who are quick-tempered are also selfish. Adjectives f and g, 'quick-tempered' and 'willing to please', have a matching score of 2. The lowest possible matching score is 0: a score of 2 indicates that, for this subject, people who are quick-tempered are unlikely to be willing to please. The next step is to convert this table of associations between pairs of adjectives into a more easily understandable form: a two-dimensional graph.

3. On your Figure 2a, mark all your matching scores of 16 or

Figure 2a

	a	b	c	d	e	f	g	h	i	j	k	l		i	ii
a.	–														
b.		–													
c.			–												
d.				–											
e.					–										
f.						–									
g.							–								
h.								–							
i.									–						
j.										–					
k.											–				
l.												–			

Ref MS p. 26 figure 2a

Figure 2b

	Happy	Autistic	Confident	Unpredictable	Well adjusted	Quick-tempered	Willing to please	Selfish	Loving	Worrier	Understanding	Hard-working		i	ii	
	a	b	c	d	e	f	g	h	i	j	k	l		i	ii	
a. Happy	–	6	10	6	14	6	**16**	8	14	10	8	10		1	0	
b. Autistic	6	–	8	14	8	12	8	12	6	8	8	8		0	0	
c. Confident	10	8	–	10	14	12	6	10	10	**4**	10	10		1	1	Dimension 2
d. Unpredictable	6	14	10	–	**4**	**16**	**4**	**18**	8	10	8	8		4	–	Dimension 1
e. Well adjusted	14	8	14	**4**	–	6	12	**4**	14	6	14	10		2	–	Dimension 1
f. Quick-tempered	6	12	12	**16**	6	–	**2**	**18**	6	8	6	10		3	–	Dimension 1
g. Willing to please	**16**	8	6	**4**	12	**2**	–	**4**	12	12	14	10		4	–	Dimension 1
h. Selfish		12	10	**18**	**4**	**18**	**4**	–	8	10	6	8		4	–	Dimension 1
i. Loving	14	6	10	8	14	6	12	8	–	12	12	10		0	0	
j. Worrier	10	8	**4**	10	6	8	12	10	12	–	10	10		1	1	Dimension 2
k. Understanding	8	8	10	8	14	6	14	6	12	10	–	10		0	0	
l. Hard-working	10	8	10	8	10	10	10	8	10	10	10	–		0	0	

larger or 4 or smaller. These are associations which are statistically significant, i.e. unlikely to be due merely to chance.

4. Count the number of marked matching scores for each adjective a–l. Enter these in column i. Pick one of the adjectives with the highest number of marked scores: this is the core adjective for the first dimension. In Figure 2b adjectives d, g and h all have four matches: d has been chosen as the core adjective.

5. Make a list consisting of the core adjective and all the adjectives which have a marked matching score with it. In Figure 2b, the adjectives are d,e,f,g and h. These adjectives are associated together in your mind and will form the first dimension of your graph. In the case of the subject in the example, 'unpredictable', 'quick-tempered' and 'selfish' are at one end of the dimension; 'well-adjusted' and 'willing to please' are at the other.

6. Remove these adjectives from the table by putting a line through them both horizontally and vertically.

7. For the remaining adjectives, count the number of matching scores which remain. Enter these in column ii.

8. Pick one of the adjectives with the highest score in column ii: this is the core adjective for the second dimension. In Figure 2b, adjective c has been picked.

9. Make a list consisting of that adjective and all the others in column ii with which it has marked matching scores: these form your second dimension. For the subject in the example, 'confident' is at one end of this dimension and 'a worrier' is at the other.

10. The next step is to calculate for each individual (1–20) a score on each dimension. Take the core adjective of dimension 1. Assign to it, and to all the other adjectives in that dimension with which it has a high marked matching score, a '+' sign. Assign to the other adjectives in that dimension, with which the core adjective has a low marked matching score, a '−' sign.

11. Take individual 1 (yourself). Look at the pattern of

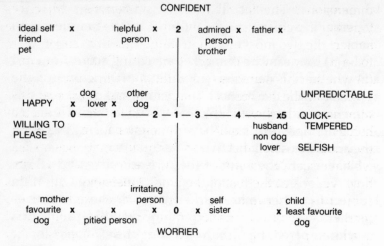

Figure 3

crosses and blanks which you have assigned to that individual for the adjectives on dimension 1. For each cross against a '+' adjective and each blank against a '−' adjective, score 1. The total is the score for individual 1 for dimension 1.

12. Repeat step 11 for each individual 2–20.

13. For scores for each individual on dimension 2, repeat steps 10 to 12, using the adjectives making up dimension 2.

14. You can now draw a graph, like the one shown in Figure 3, to show the positions of individuals in your internal world: draw two axes at right angles to each other.

15. The horizontal axis represents Dimension 1. At one end is 0, the lowest possible score for an individual on that dimension. At the other end put the highest possible score: in the example, it is 5. Do the same with the vertical axis which represents Dimension 2. The position of each individual on the two axes can then be plotted.

Interpretation of the scores

Because each person's grid is unique, there are no hard and fast rules for interpreting it. But here are some guide lines:

1. Look at the adjectives which make up the two

dimensions. The fact that you group certain adjectives together in a cluster can be revealing. In the example, to the subject the two most important things about a person seem to be (1) how easy he is to get along with (Dimension 1) and (2) whether he is anxious or confident (Dimension 2).

2. Look at the position of your mother and father on the dimensions. In the example, mother and father are seen as being at opposite ends of both dimensions, i.e. as unlike as they could possibly be. This is not uncommon, because, as we have seen, the way we see our parents tends to define how we look at the rest of the world. It also looks as if this subject finds her father harder to get along with than her mother. As well as being seen as unpredictable, selfish and quick-tempered, he is seen as having the same personality as 'person not trusted'. This difficulty seems to some extent to apply to men in general: brother and spouse are seen as similar to father.

3. Look at the positions of yourself and your ideal self. The subject in the example would ideally like to combine the good qualities of both father and mother: willing to please and confident. In reality, she sees herself as more similar to mother, though not so much of a worrier.

4. Look at the positions of favourite and least favourite dog. In the example, the subject seems to love her favourite dog because she is like her mother. Her least favourite dog is opposite to her ideal self, both unpredictable and lacking in confidence. To the subject, he is like a child.

5. As well as telling you something about your relationships with your dogs, the grid may also tell you something about the kind of dog you would get on best with. The subject in the example does not seem to mind nervous dogs, but she does not seem to like dogs who are dominant, who are intent on doing what they want rather than on pleasing her.

Part II
Aspects of Love

3 ● *Dog as Child*

'Married with two Dobes' was how one owner described herself to me. That dogs are child substitutes is by now almost a cliché, one which many owners are happy to fall in with. Julian Clary described to the magazine *Dogs Today* how he acquired his small mongrel Fanny from a pet shop in Eltham:

> *She was in a tiny cage and completely hysterical; a frantic creature who, as soon as you let her out, ran round and round in circles going to the toilet at the same time so you got a Catherine Wheel effect. I felt all these paternal instincts and wanted to father children, but that didn't seem very likely so I got Fanny instead. I instantly felt better.*

Sometimes these child substitutes are idealised, like Elizabeth Barrett Browning's little spaniel 'Flushie', of whom more later; sometimes they are perceived in more realistic terms. One owner described Sherry, a 'shaggy terrier, possibly Jack Russell/Australian cross?', who was run over by a car at the age of three. She was a difficult dog, 'snappy, inclined to wet while greeting people, bad habit of nipping edge of carpet, often pulling long threads'. But the owner has been surprised to find her popping up regularly in her dreams, 'walking on hind legs, occasionally wearing a tutu and seeming to be my daughter aged about four'.

Those scornful of the 'babyfying' of dogs sometimes imply that it is a product of our modern affluent Western society. But it is certainly not an exclusively modern phenomenon. In Chaucer's *Canterbury Tales* the Prioress, Madam Eglentyne,

> Of smale houndes hadde she that she fedde
> With rosted flessh, or milk and wastel-breed
> But soore wepte she if oon of hem were deed
> Or if men smoot it with a yerde smerte.

The idea of dogs as children has also been seized upon by scientists of various kinds. Linguists have demonstrated similarities in the ways in which people talk to their dogs and talk to their children. Adults use shorter, more grammatical sentences when talking to children than when talking to other adults. They also use the present tense more, ask more questions and give more orders. The researchers found that owners talked to dogs in the same way. The only characteristic of child-directed speech which did not apply to dogs was statements like 'this is a typewriter' or 'that is dangerous' – statements aimed at teaching them things. Owners did not do this to dogs.

Biologists have argued that, in mammals, the young of a species have certain physical characteristics which trigger a mothering response in the adult: soft skin or fur, short limbs and big heads with large eyes and small mouth and nose. They also argue that the breeds of dog most likely to be 'babied', such as Cavalier King Charles spaniels, possess these characteristics to a greater degree than other breeds.

Psychologists have tested out this child substitute idea by giving a Kelly grid, like the one described in Chapter 2, to thirty owners of pets, of which the majority were dogs or cats. When they analysed the results, they found, not surprisingly, that, on average, the relationship most similar to each subject's relationship with their pet was their relationship with their previous pet. But the next most similar relationship was, again on average, that with the subject's own child. I find this result surprising because the owners who did the Kelly grids which I sent them saw their dogs as similar to a whole range of people: father, mother and self as well as child. It may be that in this other study the process of averaging the grids reduced them to this rather boring cliché.

This cliché, however, needs to be explored further. When an owner says her dog is like a child to her, she does not mean that she treats it exactly like a child or that she cannot tell the difference, although occasionally owners behave as if confused about the difference. Elizabeth Barrett Browning tried to teach her Flushie to count so that he could eventually play dominoes with her: she didn't get very far.

> Also I once saw a 'problem' Jack Russell terrier bitch owned by a rather strange lady with long hair, wearing an ethnic dress and carrying a baby in a sling. The problem was that the dog growled at the baby when he crawled towards her bed; this was reasonable enough, but the strangeness started when she said that the dog would 'burst into tears' if left outside a shop. I asked what she meant but she looked puzzled, so I left it at that. Later she said that she thought the dog must be very intelligent because she had learned to work the washing machine.

But most of us are quite clear that our dogs are not really children. Rather, they fill the same role as children: they are dependent on us and need us to look after them. Most dogs are good at filling this role because their needs seem so easy to satisfy. 'Easy to please', 'wonderful', 'accepts any situation my life brings her into', were typical questionnaire comments about favourite dogs. Predictably, many owners commented that this feeling of being a parent to the dog was enhanced if they had bred the dog and had therefore known him from birth, especially if they had hand-reared him.

This raises the question of why people should want

someone dependent on them: why should this be a source of satisfaction rather than a nuisance. The answer lies in the early childhood scenarios. All tiny babies are absolutely dependent on their parents for their physical needs (food, warmth, etc.) and their emotional needs (comfort, cuddles, etc.). Because we live in an imperfect world, these needs are never absolutely met for anyone. A mother cannot always be there when her baby wants her and when she is there, she cannot always satisfy his needs: she may not have enough milk; she may not be able to soothe away the pain in his tummy; or she may not be able to puzzle out what it is he wants. And even when all needs are met, when a baby is blissfully comfortable and happy in his mother's arms, this idyllic state of affairs has to come to an end. Babies have to be weaned, baby brothers and sisters are born and take their place: they have to leave mother and go out to face a wider world. So all of us leave babyhood with feelings of longings unfulfilled and paradise lost. One way of dealing with this dissatisfaction and loss is to be an 'ideal parent' to someone else: create for him a blissful life, where all his needs are met. We can then enjoy and share vicariously in his feeling of complete satisfaction.

Being an ideal parent to a baby isn't as gratifying as being the baby yourself. But it has one great advantage: you are in control. If you are the baby, you are in a position of immense insecurity, because the parent can leave you at any time: if you are the parent, you can keep the scenario going as long as you want.

As we have seen, most dogs are ideal babies for this scenario, because their needs are so easily met. The 'least favourite' dogs are much more like human beings in this regard: huffy, moody, hard to please.

> *Cat-like, solitary, aloof. She does not need me, even for feeding. She will dig up root veg and pick apples when hungry. (Cocker spaniel)*

She (German shepherd) is very remote, extremely self-contained, never gives or accepts affection unless it's on her terms. Basically because she will not allow you to be close, she reminds me of an autistic child who cannot be reached. It is very sad, but we have tried so many things and failed which is something I hate to admit.

This bitch (German shepherd) was a rescue. Very clinging, very affectionate but disliked (or feared) being fussed. Seemed unable to solve basic problems like how to come in out of the rain.

There is a poem by Frances Cornford which, for me, vividly expresses how a relationship with a dog can recapture this blissful mother–baby closeness; also the feeling of desolation when the relationship is severed. The poem teeters on the verge of sentimentality but, for me, stays just on the right side of it. In it, the dog and the owner each play both parts: both are the parent and both are the child. This illustrates a point which crops up again and again when examining owner–dog relationships (or any kind of relationship for that matter). The dog is not one thing only for the owner. He is not just a parent or just a child, he is many things all at once.

A CHILD'S DREAM

I had a little dog and my dog was very small;
He licked me in the face and he answered to my call;
Of all the treasures that were mine, I loved him best of all.

His nose was fresh as morning dew and blacker than the night;
I thought that it could even snuff the shadows of the night;
And his tail he held bravely, like a banner in a fight;

His body covered thick with hair was very good to smell;
His little stomach underneath was pink as any shell;
And I loved him and honoured him, more than words can tell;

We ran out in the morning, both of us, to play;
Up and down across the fields for all the summer day;
But he ran so swiftly, he ran far away.

I looked for him, I called for him, entreatingly. Alas,
The dandelions could not speak, though they had seen him pass;
And nowhere was his waving tail among the waving grass.

The sun sank low – I ran, I prayed: 'If God has not the power
To find him, let me die. I cannot bear another hour.'
When suddenly I came upon a great yellow flower.

And all among its petals, such was Heaven's grace,
In that golden hour, in that golden place,
All among its petals, was his hairy face.

For many owners, feeding is a natural way to mother their dogs. Problems of feeding, sleeping and crying dominate the lives of mothers of tiny babies, because tiny babies cannot do much more than feed, sleep and cry: mothers realise that the most important of these is feeding. A baby can be wakeful and cry a lot, but as long as he is feeding properly, there is nothing seriously wrong. When he goes off his food, then mothers (and doctors) get really worried. And feeding is a barometer of more than physical health. If a baby feels insecure in his relationship with his mother, this first shows itself in feeding difficulties.

Because feeding is central to the relationship between a tiny baby and his mother, mothers often keep on worrying about their children's eating habits, when it has ceased to be appropriate. Two-year-olds often express their budding autonomy by adopting idiosyncratic feeding habits: never eating set meals, refusing everything except chocolate and baked beans, for example. This kind of behaviour is normal and healthy. When I held a discussion group for mothers and toddlers, the problem which most often preoccupied the mothers was food. As their obviously healthy two-year-olds raced around the room, they would enquire anxiously how they could make them eat the food that was put in front of them or make them eat at meal times. The answer was of course that they couldn't, but they found this hard to accept, because they still felt that feeding was a barometer of their relationship with their children. If the children wouldn't eat what they gave them, then they felt there must be something badly wrong.

Dogs are usually ideal 'babies' for owners who like to mother with food. Dogs are opportunistic omnivores who by instinct eat what they can get, as opposed to, for example, cats, who are fussy carnivores. They are also programmed by instinct to eat enormous amounts at one go, in case they cannot find any more food for some time. A previously well-nourished dog can survive for up to a month without food, as long as he has water. All this means that dogs are usually easy to feed. As far as most dogs are concerned, most commercial dog foods are perfectly acceptable. Manufacturers do not tinker around with their dog foods to make them more appetising to the dog, but to make them more appealing to the owner. Many owners feel they cannot be feeding their dogs properly if the food does not correspond to their idea of what a dog would like. They feel much happier if they feed him something which looks like 'meaty chunks' than something which looks like hamster food or red rubbery worms.

There are, however, dangers in being a food-centred owner. The most obvious one is that the dog gets fat. One vet reported a piece of research which purported to show that overweight dogs had overweight owners: but, as he does not seem to have weighed the owners, this must be based on his own impressions, rather than solid evidence. However, it does seem likely that owners who excessively mother their dogs with food do the same to themselves.

Another pitfall is spending too much time, trouble and money over the dog's food. Many owners prefer to prepare their dogs' food from basic ingredients: opening a tin doesn't seem personal enough. Breeders in particular, I have noticed, are prone to this, preparing their own recipes from sometimes rather revolting ingredients, such as tripe or dubious-smelling mince from pet shops. The benefits of this practice cannot be financial, as commercial dog food can be bought cheaply in bulk. It seems rather to be due to the feeling that what a dog eats is crucial to its health and appearance; and they certainly don't want to give away the responsibility for these important things to some commercial company. If ordinary pet owners make up their own recipes, they seem to favour human food, such as fish, chicken or scrambled eggs.

Often feeding dogs fancy food is a harmless hobby. But sometimes owners can paint themselves into a corner: they may inadvertently teach the dog to be fussy and accept only a limited menu. This seems specially likely if the dog is inclined to dominance (see below). Elizabeth Barrett Browning seems to have got herself into this kind of situation with Flush, although she seems to have thoroughly enjoyed it.

> *My Flush . . . will not touch the very best soup you would offer him or a potatoe unless mashed with cream and butter. At my dinner he generally tries the potatoe; and if they happen not to be cooked with what he considers the sufficient quantity of cream and butter, nobody can persuade him to take another mouthful. The only thing he never refuses, is spunge-cake, and roast partridge – yet he did refuse the latter twice in my recollection . . . when it was tough. Happily for him and the house expenses, he has a very small appetite.*

Also, these owner-prepared recipes are often too high in protein. Sometimes, of course, dogs have genuine digestive difficulties which necessitate a special diet. I hope this was really the case with Sweetie, described in the following letter to me:

> *I just had to write to you about my wee 'Sweetie', she is a mongrel and 12 years old, she was the runt of a litter and has not been really well all her life. I got her 3 weeks after my Husband died, she was only five weeks old, I am 62 years of age and only have the State pension of £53 a week and Sweetie costs me £12 a week to keep, as she can only eat chicken, white fish and rice because she has a weak stomach, but I don't grudge a penny of it as long as I have her here beside me. I have a great*

Vet called Miss Hay and as I have to take Sweetie to her nearly once or twice a month sometimes more if she is really ill, she lets me pay my account at £2 a week, I am so very grateful to her. Sweetie could never go on a bus as she would be sick after about 3 stops and I would not put my wee darling through that. I have told my Vet that when Sweetie has to get put down, she can put me down too, as I would not want to live without her.

Very rarely, an owner's worry about her dog's feeding habits may stop it eating altogether.

A young Irish vet at the Veterinary School asked me to have a look at Honey, a nine-month-old miniature long-haired dachshund who had been admitted to the hospital the previous week. She was suffering from a suspected heart murmur and had a poor appetite. All the cardiac tests had proved normal and she seemed perfectly healthy, but was still refusing to eat. When I went to see her, she turned out to be an enchanting little dog, about the size of a weasel, but much prettier, with a long silky brown coat. When the nurse and I opened her cage, she ran out to meet us. My instinctive reaction was to pick her up and she immediately snuggled against my shoulder. Apparently this had been the nurses' instinctive reaction too and they had been carrying her around like this all week, trying to tempt her with little bits of food. I asked to see her with some food in a dish and this turned out to be an extraordinary performance. She made little lunges at the dish, darting forward, as if it might bite, and then quickly retreating to a safe distance. She eventually managed to tip the dish over. She then picked up a lump of meat, but, instead of eating it, hid it under her blanket.

It looked to me as if Honey was not a dog with poor appetite: she was in a conflict about eating, wanting and being afraid to eat at the same time. It seemed likely that paying attention to this performance and, in particular, pressing food on her were probably making things worse. I suggested that we try putting down a bowl of liquid convalescent food (so that she could not hide bits under her bedding and lose them) and ignore her.

To begin with, she started her darting, lunging performance and kept running up to us. But gradually, as she got no response from us, she calmed down and eventually started to lap the food. As a result of this demonstration, the nurses changed their tactics. They did not carry her around any more and at meal times they just put down her dish and left her to it. By the end of the week, she was eating much better and had even put on some weight.

It was obviously important to see the owner and get to the bottom of what was going on, otherwise when Honey went home, she was likely to relapse. The Irish vet had mentioned vaguely that the owner was a foreign lady, whose English was hard to understand: I imagined her large-bosomed, Italian and hysterical. The reality was quite different. Miss H was a little Highland woman, dressed in a felt hat and tweed coat. She was a retired nanny and obviously her former charges formed a kind of extended family for her: one of them was driving her the 300-mile round trip necessary to pick Honey up. I never really did get to the bottom of how she and Honey had managed to get into such a muddle over food. Certainly Honey's difficulties provided a great deal of social contact with her neighbours: by her account, they seemed to be always popping in with some new delicacy, such as a home-baked rock cake, to try to tempt her. Honey was clearly the centre of her owner's life: maybe a wish to give her anything she wanted had alternated with a nannyish insistence that she eat everything that was put before her, in a way which Honey found confusing.

Whatever had gone on in the past, Honey's owner listened obediently to my instructions: Honey was to have set meal times, when her owner could give her anything she thought Honey might like. But she was to leave Honey alone with her food dish and whatever food remained uneaten after quarter of an hour was to be removed and no other food offered until the next meal.

I had a happy phone call from Miss H a week later. Honey was on the same bizarre diet of shepherd's pie, rock cakes and other donations from the neighbourhood, but – the main thing – she was eating quite well. Then, a week after that, the crisis came. Miss H telephoned me in a panic to say that Honey had not eaten for two days. I sensed that this was some kind of turning point. I thought it likely that it was in this kind of situation in the past –

when Honey went temporarily off her food – that the slide
into neurosis had begun: helped, perhaps, by the question
of the heart murmur raised by the local vet. I told Miss H
to check with her vet but that I thought that as long as
Honey had enough to drink, there was no cause for alarm.
I told her that it was important to keep Honey on the
same feeding regime: she was not to show Honey that she
was worried and she was certainly not to try to tempt
Honey to eat. I waited in some suspense for Miss H's next
phone call a few days later. Fortunately, the news was
good: after two days' fast, Honey had started to eat again
normally.

So if you are an owner who likes to mother her dog with
food, what should you do to avoid problems? If you have a
greedy dog, make sure that he doesn't get too fat. Regular
weighing is often helpful, as it can be hard to spot weight-
gain in someone you are with constantly. If he is putting on
too much weight, you will have to control the calories in his
diet, as with a human slimmer. You may find it useful to do
this in consultation with your vet; it is essential if your dog
is grossly overweight. You may find commercial dog
slimming foods useful. Although more expensive, they
provide a balanced diet with fewer calories for the same
bulk, so that you do not have to give your dog insultingly
minute amounts of food at each meal. Like a human
weight-watcher, your dog is allowed low-calorie foods,
such as fruit and vegetables ad-lib, so that you can still
share your elevenses with your dog as long as he gets a
carrot rather than a biscuit. (Perhaps you should be eating
a carrot too?)

For dogs who are worryingly fussy about their food, use
the regime advocated for Miss H and Honey: give him food
you think he will eat, but (unless he is a puppy) offer it only
twice a day, at a regular time. Leave him alone with his
food and remove the dish after fifteen minutes. Once he is
eating reliably, if the food is inappropriate nutritionally
and/or expensive, you should mix in with it gradually
increasing quantities of commercial dog food.

Owners wondering whether to have their bitches spayed are sometimes worried because they have heard that it may make them fat. Vets often reassure them that this can easily be prevented by feeding fewer calories. But it is not as simple as that, especially for food-orientated owners. In a research project into the behavioural effects of spaying on bitches, I found that one of the few significant effects was to make spayed bitches greedier: they ate more quickly, they were less fussy about what they ate and they tended to look for snacks between meals in the form of carrion, rubbish, etc. This change could be beneficial for a fussy eater, but not for an already greedy one.

Another result of attaching emotional importance to food is the fashionable tendency to try to cure behavioural problems by changing a dog's diet. The myth that junk food can make children behave badly has been around for some years, in spite of the fact that there have been no controlled studies to prove it. On the contrary, in a recent study of children whose parents thought they were affected by food additives, it was found that when neither the children nor the parents knew when the children were getting additives in their food and when they weren't, only a tiny percentage turned out genuinely to be reacting to the additives.

More recently, the same idea has entered the dog world. Most animal behaviourists, including myself, have seen at least one or two cases where a change of diet seems to have brought about a change of behaviour.

A young couple, Mr and Mrs E, brought a nine-month-old Great Dane puppy, Eustace, to see me. They said he was generally very nervous and spent most of his time at home trembling behind the sofa. Someone dropping a newspaper or a tea towel would scare him out of his wits. Although he seemed pretty nervous in the consultation which he spent sitting on Mr A's knee (quite an acrobatic feat) they said he had improved markedly over the past two weeks: they had been feeding Eustace red meat only (a wildly unsuitable diet nutritionally) and their vet had recommended that they change to a commercial dog food.

But this kind of anecdotal evidence can be misleading: when a dog's diet is changed in these circumstances, other things are usually altered too. Dietary change is often recommended as part of a whole new regime; even when it is recommended on its own, the owner's attitude is bound to change in some way, even if it is only to become more hopeful. Until a controlled study is done, the question of whether diet can affect a dog's behaviour must remain open. In the meantime, although it can do no harm to experiment with diet, this seems likely to be worthwhile only if the deterioration in behaviour coincides with a change in diet or if the diet is unsuitable nutritionally. In addition, diet could affect only general disorders of temperament: nervousness, hyperactivity or irritability. It could not possibly affect behaviour problems which occur only in a specific situation: a fear of thunderstorms or a tendency to attack men in uniform, for example.

Mothering owners gratify their dogs' wants and needs in ways other than feeding. Most of these needs are very easy to gratify. Most dogs want to be in their owners' company; they want to be patted, cuddled and talked to; they enjoy being taken for a walk; they enjoy having a game with a ball or stick. Sometimes owners take pleasure in meeting more unusual demands. J. M. Barrie writes of Thomas Hardy:

> *Once when I was at Dorchester, he showed me a letter from a firm which had presented him with a broadcasting set. They said they were delighted to hear from him that it gave pleasure but that they were rather damped to learn from another source that it was not he who listened but his dog. This was quite true.*
>
> *We went that afternoon to a local rehearsal of the play of Tess, and the dog, who was with us, behaved beautifully until the time came when he knew the wirelesss would be putting on the Children's Hour. It was his favourite item. He howled for it so that even Tess's champion had to desert her and hurry home with him. The dog afterwards discovered that a weather report, or*

*something of the kind, was issued in the early morning, and I
understand his master used to go down stairs in the cold and
turn it on for him.*

In most cases, there is no harm in 'indulging' a dog in this
way; it gives both dog and owner a great deal of pleasure.
However, if the dog is inclined to dominance (for a fuller
account of dominance and its treatment see *Problem Dog*) it
will lead to problems. Like their wild ancestors, wolves,
dogs are instinctively programmed to live in a hierarchical
pack, with a leader. For a pet dog, this pack is its human
family.

Some dogs have a strong instinct to become a pack
leader: these dogs will make a bid for dominance by
constantly testing out the other pack members: they will
constantly take the initiative and ask them for things. If the
owner complies with these demands, the dog assumes that
the owner has accepted subordinate status and that he, the
dog, is dominant. If this happens, problems are likely to
arise sooner or later, when the owner steps out of his
subordinate role. For example, some dominant dogs
become aggressive when their owners pat them (a dominant gesture), try to turn them off the furniture or give
them an unwelcome command.

Mr & Mrs B came to consult me about their Springer
spaniel, Bobby. Their problem was a doggy variant of the
common step-parent/step-child problem. Mr B had
married Mrs B and Bobby a year ago and had moved into
their house. Mrs B, plump, confident and bouncy, went
out to work each day. Mr B, thin, pale and apprehensive,
was unemployed and stayed behind with Bobby.
Understandably, when he first moved in, he had tried to
make himself agreeable to his wife's beloved dog, by
responding to his demands for play, walks, etc. The
results were disastrous. The dog, confirmed in his
position as man of the house, instituted a tyrannical
regime. Mr B could move around the house during the
day, as long as Bobby followed him. But if he tried to
leave the house without Bobby, he was bitten. If he tried

to have a meal without sharing it with Bobby, he was attacked. At night, Bobby slept at the foot of their bed and bit him if he tried to get up. Showing any physical affection towards Mrs B was, of course, completely forbidden.

This is the most extreme case of dominance aggression I have seen. They only came to see me once: Mr B rang to cancel the next appointment, saying enigmatically that 'things have changed'. I hope that what he meant was that he had forced his wife to choose between him and Bobby.

Many more dogs are dominant without showing such spectacular aggression, or even showing any aggression towards people at all. Like Thomas Hardy's dog, they may merely issue a series of demands throughout the day and make a nuisance of themselves if these demands are not met. Some of these dogs go on to show aggression eventually. Others just remain a moderate nuisance because they will not do what the owner tells them.

Some dogs show their dominance in bizarre ways. A young couple, Mr & Mrs J, consulted me about their Staffordshire bull terrier, Jock. The trouble started when they were out for a walk one day near some slag heaps. While chasing a rabbit, Jock came across a part of the slag heap which was still smouldering and burnt his feet and under-side. The Js rushed him to the vet for emergency treatment. He was in great pain, but after some weeks of careful nursing by the Js, he made a full physical recovery. But, when they started to take him out for walks again, he vomited. At home, he was energetic and seemed perfectly healthy. The only time he was sick there was if he played with another dog. The vet could find nothing the matter with him. Thinking that his walks aroused frightening memories of his traumatic experience, they tried different outings, in another direction. He was still sick. They tried not taking him for a walk: he pestered them and made life generally unbearable until they took him out again. Also, he showed no signs of fear on the walks: he did not tremble, whine or try to go home.

It seemed to me that his home life was that of a very

dominant dog, continually asking his owners for things and always getting them. I wondered if things were different on the walks. Sure enough, Mr J said that he, rather than Jock, decided the routes of the walks: they would go to buy a newspaper or eggs from a neighbouring farm. Mr J continually had to call Jock, not because he was slow but because he would potter off in another direction, investigating things. I wondered if Jock's vomiting was an expression of conflict over dominance. Maybe he resented being bossed about but didn't want to get left behind either. This would also explain why he was sick when other dogs visited: they posed a threat to his dominance.

To test out this theory, we took him for a walk in the courtyard of the Veterinary School. First of all, Mr J allowed him to go where he wanted: he trotted around at a fairly energetic pace, investigating interesting smells. The Js and I scurried along behind, with me trying to focus on Jock with a video camera. Then I asked Mr J to walk away from him and call him. He tore himself away from a piece of orange peel he was sniffing, walked a few yards and was sick. 'Oh good,' I exclaimed as the camera whirred; and 'Clever boy,' shouted Mr J. A group of passing students looked very puzzled.

I suggested that the Js treat the problem by restructuring their relationship with Jock so that he no longer saw himself as the dominant one in the family (see *Problem Dog*). To begin with, on walks, Jock was to be allowed to decide the pace and route; then, gradually, the Js were to start to assert their dominance on walks as well. A week or two later they reported that Jock, though not completely recovered, was vomiting much less often.

If you are like the Js or Thomas Hardy and enjoy gratifying your dog's wishes, you should try to choose a dog who is unlikely to be dominant. The guarding breeds and small terriers are to be avoided. Male dogs are more likely to be dominant than females. Castration may reduce the dominance of a male dog but spaying may increase dominance in an already dominant bitch.

To return to the subject of food, I have noticed that many dominant dogs are fussy eaters. The most likely reason for this seems to be that, rather than eating it, these dogs use their food to assert their dominant status. For example, they may be preoccupied with guarding it and keeping other people away from it. Or, as mentioned above, they may even refuse it in order to get something nicer.

The results of a study which I carried out in 1984 are relevant here. The study was funded by a pet food company, who were about to launch a new dried dog food and wanted to know what kind of owners were likely to buy it. So I interviewed fifty dog owners and asked them a peculiar combination of questions. I asked them about what their dogs ate, about their dogs' behaviour and about their own behaviour and attitudes towards their dogs. (I also asked them to fill in a questionnaire which measured how neurotic they were; more about that later.) When I analysed the results statistically, I found that the owners' attitudes towards their dogs could be described in terms of two factors or dimensions (rather like the Kelly grids in Chapter 2). The first dimension was one of attachment: there were owners who were extremely attached to their dogs, who missed them very much when they were separated from them and felt they would be very upset if they died. And there were owners who did not seem very attached to their dogs: they did not mind being parted from them and they did not expect to be upset when they died.

Independent of that dimension was a dimension which I called 'anthropomorphic emotional involvement'. The emotionally involved owners liked their dogs to be loving and dependent on them; they also tended to feed their dogs tit-bits and let them sleep in their bedrooms. At the other end of the dimension were tough-minded owners, who were no less attached to their dogs, but did not like them to be dependent. The emotionally attached owners would probably fit into this section of the book somewhere, seeing their dogs as children, parents, lovers, etc. The tough-minded owners would probably belong to Chapter 7.

I was surprised to find that the owners' feeding habits fitted quite neatly into this system. Non-attached owners tended to feed tinned commercial dog food. Emotionally attached owners tended to feed specially prepared food such as chicken, fish or scrambled egg. The only ones who used dried dog food were the tough-minded owners, a result which didn't please the pet food company much. The dogs' behaviour was also linked to owner attitudes and food. Dogs showing dominant behaviour towards their owners were more likely to be owned by emotionally attached owners. They were also more likely than other dogs to be fed on chicken, scrambled egg, etc. As discussed earlier, it seems unlikely that the food was affecting their temperament directly: more likely that the diet was the result of the interaction between a dominant dog and an emotionally involved owner.

So far, this chapter has dealt with owners who enjoy mothering their dogs. But there are other owners who are repelled by dogs who behave like babies. For example one owner wrote of her Chinese crested bitch: 'She is neurotic and hyperactive and clinging. I like a dog to not be dependent on me but do its own thing.' These are the 'tough-minded' owners of the questionnaire. Another such owner described her favourite dog, a German shepherd, as 'loyal, obedient and intelligent'. Her least favourite, Jess, a collie-cross 'constantly seeks attention i.e. jumps onto my lap furiously licking my face and pawing at my hands. She would do this constantly, if I didn't stop her. She persists even when I do cuddle and stroke her and never settles down to lie quietly on my lap or by my side to have her tummy rubbed, etc. I have had her since she was nine months old and three weeks pregnant (immediately spayed). She originally belonged to some local Asian shop keepers who asked me to have her (assuring me that she had not yet been in season!) I joke that her disobedience is due to her only understanding Hindi!' (I think that the unconscious significance of the link between the dog and

Indian culture is that, in Indian families, dependence in young children is expected and enjoyed.)

These owners often feel that their own mother's mothering was unsatisfactory. The owner of Jess describes her own mother as 'over-protective: she shows her affection by over-feeding and worrying about those she loves'. She has a 'love/hate' relationship with her and also says, 'I do not get maternal feelings about children and have never wanted babies.'

If you know you feel like this about dogs, you should try to avoid the more dependent breeds, such as spaniels. One of the small Scottish terriers (e.g. cairn, West Highland white) would probably suit you better. If you already have a dog who is annoyingly dependent, then one solution might be to find him another home with a mothering owner.

4 ● *Dog as Parent*

Dogs can be parents as well as children. The idea may seem strange but it has a long history: one example is the legend of Romulus and Remus and, more recently, Nana Darling in J. M. Barrie's *Peter Pan*.

The most obvious parental job a dog does is to protect his owners. In an Australian survey of 1,000 owners, 27% felt that protection was one benefit of owning a dog. Often owners feel protected merely by the dog's presence, like the girl answering my questionnaire who said, 'My parents didn't mind me being out in the dark as much when I had Suzie (a German shepherd) with me and I know I myself felt safer.' Sometimes it is more actively protective:

> *My dog Tyson had to be put to sleep last year, it has affected my ability to ever have a bull terrier again. He protected me whilst my (lorry driver) husband was away. He was totally reliable with me, he was, however, unreliable with other people. He didn't care for children or men. He always knew when I felt threatened and reacted to it by threatening the threatener without any prompting from me.*

The subject of dangerous dogs is dealt with more fully in Chapter 9, but there is a particular potential danger in giving a dog the role of a protective parent. Part of a parent's protective function is to decide what is really dangerous and what isn't, because children can't do this. They may be afraid of Auntie who is blind and not afraid of the friendly stranger who invites them into his car for some sweeties. Dogs may sometimes seem to their owners to be better than they are at spotting the person who is up to no good. Like Tyson they are presumably very sensitive to subtle inconsistencies in the person's body language. But they can also make mistakes.

> Mrs R came to consult me about Rusty, a middle-sized, sandy-haired mongrel who looked rather like a dingo. Mrs R was fat and cheerful, with dyed hair and bad teeth. She looked as if she ran a pub, but in fact she ran an old people's home. Rusty was popular with the residents. He was also a comfort to the dying, sitting quietly for long periods by their bedsides. The trouble was that he had become over-protective of his charges. He challenged any strangers he met in the corridors. Initially Mrs R felt this was quite useful, but when he started to go for people like the locum GP, she felt matters were getting out of hand. Also, death-bed vigils seemed to make him particularly protective. He was sitting by the bedside of a dying resident, when her daughter arrived and sat down too. They both sat there quite calmly until the daughter opened her handbag. For some reason this did not meet with Rusty's approval and he growled and barked until the daughter left the room. Mrs R felt that this kind of incident did the reputation of the home no good.

Another example of over-protection is the behaviour of a rare breed of terrier. I deliberately refrain from specifying the breed because I was approached by the breed society which, commendably, was trying to improve its temperament. To find out more about the problem, they had sent questionnaires to owners and they asked me for my opinion about the replies. These showed that when any of these dogs had a behaviour problem it was often the same specific one: the dog would protect the owner against someone he saw as threatening; thereafter, he seemed to develop an *idée fixe* about that kind of person and show protective aggression every time he met one. So one of them would always attack boys in jeans and another attacked men in navy blue uniform. As time went on, the attacks would require less and less provocation, so that some dogs would cross the road to attack their chosen kind of victim minding his own business on the other side.

Because of the abnormally high frequency of this problem in the breed, it was clear that a genetic factor was at work in these cases. But, in addition, the owner may play a part in turning his dog's protectiveness into a problem by encouraging his aggression:

> Mrs M had acquired her Border collie Mandy. Her husband worked on an oil rig and she did not feel safe alone in the house. She encouraged Mandy to bark at strangers approaching the house and at strange noises. Mandy became a problem when she started to growl and lunge at any visitor who crossed the threshold. Also the noises which caused her to bark became less and less unusual; she was up and down all night, barking at car doors slamming or noisy motor cycles. This interfered with Mr M's sleep when he was at home.
>
> Eventually he pronounced that if Mandy didn't stop barking at night, she would have to go. At this point, Mrs M consulted me. Unfortunately, the treatment never got off the ground because I told Mrs M that it was not reasonable to expect Mandy to distinguish between important and trivial sounds and between desirable and undesirable visitors. Any treatment programme would have to be directed at reducing all this protective activity. Mrs M just couldn't accept this.

When owners feel protected by their dogs' aggression towards strangers, they are usually construing their dogs' motivation correctly: the dog is acting out of a protective instinct. But owners sometimes see as protective actions which are nothing of the kind. In recent years one dog was given an award for rescuing his owner from the bath, after she fell into it unconscious. A similar award was won by another who discovered a toddler drowning in a rock pool and pulled him onto the beach. Although these were life-saving actions, it is doubtful whether the dogs perceived

them as such. They were both Labradors and were probably prompted by a retrieving instinct, which would have
been elicited as readily by a thrown stick or a dead bird.
Presumably these kinds of incidents are selected for
awards and publicity because a dog attacking a burglar
does not show dogs in such an unambiguously favourable
light.

Another parental characteristic of dogs is their capacity
to love their owners unconditionally. In most of our
relationships with other human beings we are aware that
their love or their friendship depends on our keeping up a
certain standard of behaviour. Our spouse or our friends
may expect us to be bright, helpful and cheerful. If we are
moody, demanding or dirty in our personal habits, they
may get fed up with us. To the extent to which we feel we
cannot be fully ourselves with someone, we feel insecure in
the relationship. But we expect our relationship with our
parents to be different: we expect them to love us no matter
what we do. When the mother of a mass murderer says to
the press, 'He's just my wee boy,' we feel she is behaving
properly. Dogs accept us unconditionally in the same way.
They do not mind if we are dirty, smelly or physically
unattractive. And once a dog has become attached to a
particular human being as owner, it is very difficult to
break that attachment. A dog who is ignored or neglected
may become depressed and a dog who is hit or shouted at a
great deal may become anxious, but he usually stays
attached to his owner, however unsatisfactory.

Some owners feel that their dogs give them even more
than unconditional love: for example, a kennel manager,
25, of a two-year-old bearded collie:

> I feel she is easily susceptible to my moods, i.e. she reassures me
> if I am upset – she seems to know what I want from her before I
> say it.

A housewife, 56, of a Labrador:

She was a very big Lab and during her time with us we had a lot of family illness and bereavement and I could pour my soul out to Jessie, hugging her close and she soaked it all up and would lick away my tears of which there were many.

A canine beautician, 38, of an eight-year-old Staffordshire bull terrier:

She is gentle. Knows when you are not feeling 100%. I think she has been here before.

What these owners are describing is something which all children need from their parents, but which is vital for very tiny babies, who cannot manage their own emotions at all. When a baby is hungry or upset, he starts to cry. If his mother does not come, he quickly gets beside himself, he is completely possessed by his own distress. When his mother arrives to comfort him, she does this by under-standing and responding to his upset state, without get-ting upset herself. It is as if she absorbs or mops up her baby's emotions. If, on the other hand, the mother herself is upset by her baby's crying, a vicious circle starts. The baby senses that his upset has made his mother anxious and at a loss. This, in its turn, adds to his anxiety and distress.

How can a dog perform this demanding function for its owner, when mothers often cannot do it for their own babies? To some extent, the owners must be deluding themselves: the dogs obviously cannot understand the nature of their owners' predicaments in the way that a sympathetic human listener can. Because the dog does not get upset or angry or go away, the owner can imagine that he understands and tolerates what he is saying, a bit like a child confiding his troubles to his teddy bear. But detailed descriptions show that dogs can respond more actively and appropriately than teddy bears.

Tiggy is a very kind dog. Shortly after she arrived I had a fall while delivering charity envelopes and staggered home with what

turned out to be a fractured cheek bone. I could do nothing but
fall into a chair with a cold compress. My other dog would have
been impatient at my inactivity – he would have pushed his nose
into my hand and whined and pawed until he got my attention.
All Tiggy did was to pad quietly up, rest her head on my knee
for a moment with an expression of what I can only describe as
utmost sympathy and curled up quietly by my feet, till my
husband came home.

It seems likely that, in this kind of case, genuine social communication is going on. Wolves often show concern if another pack member is hurt or ill. It seems reasonable to suppose that dogs do the same for their owners.

Incidentally, dogs also seem to be able to perform a similar mothering function for species other than human beings. In a rather disturbing experiment, Rhesus monkey babies were taken away from their mothers. Half of these babies were given plastic hippos covered in artificial fur. They could cling to these toys as they would to their mothers, but the toys did not move or respond in any way. The rest of the babies were provided with dogs as companions. The dogs did not try to feed or clean the monkeys, but they were tolerant and sociable. They also allowed the monkeys to cling to them. The experimenters found that the monkeys with the dog mothers grew up to be more alert and out-going than those with the plastic hippo mothers. They were more interested in their surroundings and solved problems faster.

As adults, we still need this same emotional support from time to time. Ideally, in families, parents get this from one another. This is one of the things which makes being a single parent so difficult. A man in this position writes:

At the time I acquired Jimmy (a Manchester terrier) I was
bringing up three teenage children on my own – no mean task for
a man. They all went through the normal teenage stage where I
was regarded as the enemy. I found these times extremely
depressing but Jimmy would put his head on my knee and look at
me obviously saying, 'I love you even if no one else does.' It

never failed to lift my spirits. I soon realised that if he owed me
his life – he was a rescue dog – I owed him a greater debt, my
sanity. Without him I could not have coped.

What are the pitfalls of using your dog as an emotional
sponge? If the dog is able to fill this role, there seem to be
none. But if the dog is not up to playing this part, there can
be trouble. Some dogs have personalities like Tigger in
Winnie-the-Pooh – relentlessly bouncy and cheerful, regard-
less of how people around them are feeling. A dog like this
can be a sad disappointment to his owner, if he replaces a
sympathetic dog. Fortunately, however, a dog like this is
usually impervious to his owner's disappointment and the
relationship often settles down eventually. The real trouble
occurs when the dog is so sensitive that he cannot cope
with his owner's anxiety. Then a situation arises like the
one in which the mother cannot cope with her child's
crying, in which dog and owner get more and more
worked up.

One of the many kinds of behaviour problem to which
Alsatians are prone is tail-chasing. The worst case I have
seen was Prince, who, as soon as he was let off the lead in
my consulting room, started to whirl around with the
desperation of a drug addict looking for a fix. When he
finally managed to catch hold of his tail, he stood stock
still, with a glazed look in his eyes. (The analogy with an
addict is not a fanciful one. It is now thought that
stereotypies, as these repetitive, meaningless activities are
called, produce a kind of 'high' in the brain. This theory is
supported by the finding that they can sometimes be
temporarily suppressed by morphine antagonists.) His
owner, Mrs P, looked exhausted and puffy.

Mr P had bought Prince for her when he went to work
on the oil rigs and she had felt much comforted and
protected by his presence. The tail-chasing had only
started after they came back from holiday. She blamed the
kennels they had left him in; the proprietor had had a
'funny look'. Although I was prepared to believe that
being separated from his mistress had something to do

with the problem, I thought it unlikely that this was the whole story, especially as Prince had not started tail-chasing until about a week after they had returned. And, indeed, it emerged that the Mrs P who returned from holiday was very different from the Mrs P who set out. While they were in France, she had suffered sudden and acute heart failure. She was admitted to a French hospital and had nearly died. She was now waiting for admission to a Scottish hospital for a coronary bypass.

Prince, in the state that he was in, was obviously the last thing that Mrs P needed in the state that she was in. At home, she said, she was continually up and down, distracting him, soothing him and finally losing her temper with him. In the consultation, she was beside herself. 'He's dying, he's dying,' she repeated, over and over again.

In fact, Prince looked remarkably healthy. His tail was not even damaged. But in this fear of dying lay the clue to what was going on. Prince was not dying, but Mrs P was in mortal danger and all she could do was wait for her operation. Her husband had gone back to the oil rigs. Prince was not a dog who could contain this dreadful anxiety. He had developed a stress symptom of his own. This in turn made Mrs P even more anxious and she felt him to be in the same danger as herself.

Milder forms of this kind of vicious circle of anxiety and stress are more common. In the study described in Chapter 3, in which I asked owners about their dogs' behaviour and their own behaviour and attitudes, I also gave the owners a questionnaire test of neuroticism. This contained questions like 'Are you afraid of heights?' and 'Do you worry a lot?'. It has been found to differentiate reliably between patients suffering from an anxiety neurosis and a control group. I found that the dogs of the more neurotic owners were more likely to get over-excited and to be destructive in their owners' absence (a common stereotypy). The most likely mechanism whereby the owner's anxiety is transferred to the dog is that the owner, when anxious, behaves more emotionally and more inconsistently towards his dog, alternately fussing over him and shouting at him as Mrs P did. This increases the dog's stereotypic behaviour for two reasons: firstly, the owner's crossness and inconsistency increase the dog's stress level; secondly, the extra attention paid to the behaviour acts as a reward and tends to increase it.

> So I told Mrs P that Prince was not dying, he had merely got into a bad habit. She was to ignore him when he began to chase his tail, but praise him and give him lots of attention when he stopped. I told her that this would not cure Prince overnight, but that gradually the habit would die away. Meantime, he would come to no harm. Because stereotypies are self-rewarding, they can be slow to disappear if treated by this method alone. Keeping the dog busy and distracting him is often more effective, but I felt that Mrs P was not up to an energetic and complicated treatment regime of this kind. Unfortunately, the morphine antagonists which can suppress stereotypies were at this time just being developed. They could only be given by injection and their effect lasted only twenty minutes. Nowadays, they come in tablet form and their effect lasts longer. I wonder if they would have saved Prince's life; when Mr P returned home the day after the consultation and saw Prince still whirling, he took him straight off to the vet to be destroyed.

Some owners assign to their dogs yet another parental role: providing a safe and welcoming base to come home to. Some dogs take this duty very seriously:

> *When I first started work 21 years ago [wrote a thirty-seven-year-old beauty therapist] my dog then [a mongrel] would follow me to the railway station every morning and see me off on the train. I would watch him from the carriage and see him about to turn and go home. Invariably he would be there to meet me off the train at night. We lived about 1½ miles from the station.*

Most parental dogs, however, are expected merely to wait patiently at home and be pleased to see their owners when they return. But it is unreasonable to expect even this of a dog. Dogs are by instinct pack animals and to feel secure they need to have pack members around them. Most dogs become resigned to being left alone at home, but if your dog is beside himself with excitement when you return, he has probably been anxious and stressed while you were out. Some dogs who are distressed at being left whine or bark continually or are destructive, chewing up cushions, scraping away paintwork, etc. Like tail-chasing, these are stereotypies which serve to relieve the dog's nervous tension. A behaviour problem of this kind can be treated, or, better still, prevented (see *Problem Dog*), but in order to do so, it is essential that the owner abandon any moralistic attitude towards the dog's behaviour. I used to be puzzled when owners forcefully insisted that their dog 'ought' to be capable of being left alone. Most dogs are, some dogs aren't, but there is no 'ought' about it. Then I realised that the 'ought' stemmed from a view of dog as parent. Certainly a child has a right to expect his parents to wait for him at home: they may worry about him, but they shouldn't rip the wallpaper off the walls or disembowel the sofa. Dog owners, on the other hand, have no right to expect their dogs to stay calm at home. Luckily, most dogs can tolerate owners being away for a few hours at a time, working part-time, say. But a dog is not an appropriate pet for someone who works full-time. Cats can usually tolerate these long absences much better, although, from the owners' point of view, they may not be so satisfyingly parental. They may be out on some business of their own when he comes home.

If, for some owners, their dogs embody ideal parental characteristics of a universal kind, many more perceive their dog as having a personality similar to one of their own real parents, or as making up for one of their real parents' deficiencies.

Mrs M, a woman in late middle-age with grown-up children, filled in my questionnaire and did a Kelly grid

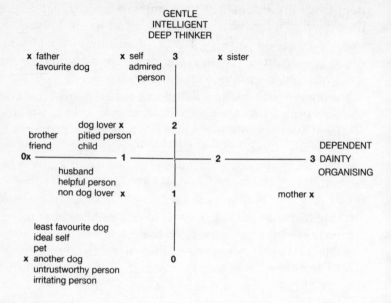

Figure 4

(Figure 4). She describes her father as a 'typical West Highlander, quiet, thoughtful and religious'. She felt she did not know him well as he was away a lot and when he was at home 'his motto seemed to be that his only child should be seen and not heard'. Her mother was a small, dainty woman, a 'talented violinist and very good at needlework'. She was also bossy and 'couldn't stand mess of any kind'. Mrs M was terrified of her. She felt she was a disappointment because she was big and messy and not interested in 'nice things'.

Her favourite dog was Mick, an Irish setter who died of cancer at the age of six. He was her favourite dog because 'he made it so obvious I was his reason for living'. He also had 'a fantastic brain and natural brilliance, very gentle, very nicely mannered, but his circle of friends was small'.

Her Kelly grid shows two main dimensions: 'intelligent, gentle, deep thinker' and 'dainty, organising, dependent'.

As you might expect, her mother is seen as extremely dainty and organising.

Her father is seen as almost as far away from mother as possible: not dainty and organising but a deep thinker. What is revealing about the grid is that Mick is exactly like father. Thus, he is special to Mrs M, not just because he was a clever dog who was devoted to her, but because he represented the father she longed for. He had her father's good qualities, but rather than being disappointingly absent, physically and psychologically, Mick was with her all the time.

With her dogs, Miss S, a kennel-maid in her thirties, seems to have recreated her family situation. What is more, what she says about her dogs offers a clue as to what went wrong in her family. Miss S has a good relationship with her mother who is 'open, bright and practical'. She is only now starting to like her father as a person. When she was a child, he was uncommunicative and she feels that the main crisis in her life was 'realising that father drank to the point where it would seriously embarrass Mum if I took school friends home. Also, money was short due to this.'

When I wrote to Miss S, I asked her if she knew why her father drank, but she could not make sense of it: 'Apparently, at work, my father was a witty man (this was told me only recently by an old workmate). As he never communicated well with us as a family, I can only assume that it was his family life that he found stressful.' However, her grid and her descriptions of her dogs throw some light on this (Figure 5). In her grid, she and her mother are seen as identical and very close to 'favourite dog'. Father and 'least favourite dog' are also similar. Her favourite, a Border collie bitch, was 'abandoned at birth and hand-reared by myself, so obviously bonded to me. I reinforced our bond by taking her everywhere with me.' Her least favourite dog is a male Labrador who is 'very intense with a lot of jealousy and ability to sulk. In his eagerness to be closest to me, he often shows disrespect to the older, disabled members of my pack – knocking them

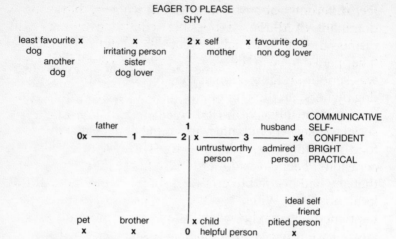

Figure 5

aside. Because he is too much of a coward to challenge others, he is sneaky in his abuse of them.'

This vivid description offers a plausible scenario of what went on in Miss S's family. Her mother had a close relationship with her children; her father, unable to establish this contact, felt left out, jealous and sulky. Not able to assert himself directly, drink was both his consolation and his 'sneaky' way of getting back at the rest of the 'pack'.

I have not seen either of these women with their dogs, but from the sound of it, both are well able to manage them. We know about the place of their dogs in their inner worlds only because they have allowed us privileged access to it. For some people, however, casting the dog in a parental role can cause a real problem. A dominant dog who is treated as a parent may well feel he has realised his ambition. Owners of parent-dogs comply with their demands, not because, like the owners of child-dogs, this gives them pleasure, but because they feel they have no right to interfere with what he decides to do. If he wants to sit on the comfiest chair, who are they to displace him? Owners who are bitten by a dominant parent-dog often feel differently about it than those who are bitten by a dominant child-dog. If possible, child-dog owners will dismiss the bite as trivial or excuse it: 'he didn't mean it' or 'I happened to be in the way'. Forced to accept that the bite was serious and intentional, they feel deeply hurt. Parent-dog owners, on the other hand, may accept the bite as due punishment for having challenged parental authority. A social worker whom I interviewed in the course of the dog-food questionnaire, admitted she had, on three or four occasions, been so badly bitten by her Scottie, Frederick, that she had needed to go the Casualty Department of the local hospital. When I asked her how these bites had happened, she said, 'I was trying to get the mud off his paws. I went too far, I should have known better.'

From an animal behaviourist point of view, this kind of problem can be hard to treat, because the owner unconsciously feels that the dog's rightful position is a dominant one.

A vet contacted me about Miss W. She wanted to refer her on to me, because she was tired of Miss W telephoning her at all hours about Yorkshire terrier William. She said she had told Miss W time and time again to be firm with William, but it seemed to make no difference. When Miss W telephoned me, she was pressing about the necessity of seeing me as soon as possible, but seemed unable to manage the times I suggested, a combination which is usually a bad sign. William, when I eventually managed to meet him, turned out to be slightly over-sized for a Yorkshire terrier ('Oh, yes, he is very big,' said Miss W), but it would still have been easy to pick him up with one hand.

William lived with Miss W and her elderly mother, who apparently doted on him. The trouble was that William had firm ideas about how Mrs and Miss W should behave. They weren't allowed to sit on certain chairs or, sometimes, to move from room to room or even, occasionally, to talk to each other. He enforced these rules by snapping at their feet and ankles. Miss W could usually outwit or evade him, but Mrs W, who was less agile both mentally and physically, was more at risk. She was also a more vulnerable target, as she liked to wear soft slippers in the house.

When I gave Miss W my standard explanation of how to establish dominance over a dominant dog – ignoring its demands, making rewards conditional on obedience – she dismissed this as if it were quite impossible. The objection did not seem to be that she could not bear to deny William anything, it was more as if my instructions were beside the point. When I suggested that, until William's behaviour had improved, her mother should wear something more impenetrable than soft slippers, she looked bothered and flustered. She left me feeling I had done little good and, sure enough, a month or two later she telephoned me to say that things were no better. A year later, she telephoned to tell me the same thing, though she did not want to come and see me again.

Pondering this series of encounters, I realised that when she told me about William's aggression towards her mother, Miss W felt as if she were telling me about rows between her parents, incidents which upset and frightened her, but in which she felt she had no business to interfere. By telling her how to interfere, I was indeed missing the point.

5 ● *Good Samaritans*

An owner answering my questionnaire wrote:

About six months previously I had my old dog put to sleep at about seventeen years of age. I never go straight out and replace my dog – one day, sooner or later, I know that it is the right day to start looking for my next dog. So when the day came, I went around one or two shelters in the vicinity, not once but several times during the next two or three weeks. I always try not to take a dog that I am sorry for – usually I am sorry for the lot anyway. In one shelter I noticed an ill-looking dog, terrible coat, bones showing everywhere, suffering from the runs and not really interested in the dogs with him in the exercise area. I am sure he didn't even notice me. It was explained that he was a cruelty case not available for adoption and I didn't think twice about him. A couple of weeks later the shelter called me up to say they thought they might have the right dog for me – a collie cross German shepherd, about nine months old, owners just starting up a business, dog couldn't be there, had to be shut away all day, etc. so needed a home. I went over to look at this dog. He was quite nice, but . . . I wasn't sure, so while I was thinking, I walked up the aisle, chatting to the dogs on one side as I went and, turning at the top, chatted to those on the other side on my way down. Near the top, I recognised Bones (as the sick dog had been nicknamed) – he didn't look much better, but when I spoke to him, he came up and stuck his nose through the bars to sniff my hand. I remember him looking at me but he didn't wag his tail or indeed show much of any feeling. I carried on down the line to look at the collie-cross again. Half way down, for what reason I shall never know, I stopped and turned around and looked back. Bones was standing on his hind legs, weak as he was, looking over the barrier at me. I must have been about thirty feet away down the building and I hadn't patted him or anything. I turned around and walked back towards him and he

dropped down and again put his nose through the bars. This time
I put my hand through and touched him gently under his chin.
Again I don't remember if he wagged his tail, certainly if he did,
it would have been the slightest twitch. I went back to the shelter
office and said that the collie cross was a very nice dog but that I
was going to have Bones. Of course there was a lot of difficulty,
but eventually I got things organised and three days later I took
him home. He was not officially adopted but still belonged to the
RSPCA. I had to guarantee to make him available for police
inspection once a month, fifteen miles away, where the case
would be heard, and visit the vet up there once a week for
weighing and examination as evidence. My own vet told me that
because of dehydration and starvation it was possible we would
never get him right. But we did: he doubled his weight and
became a happy, outgoing dog. I have had many dogs in my life,
and the one I have now is fantastic, but I have not felt so close to
any other dog.

This is a particularly striking story, but it is common for an
owner to feel especially close to a dog who has had
something wrong with him and whom the owner has
nursed or treated. There are various reasons for this. First
of all, an owner who nurses a dog is often forced to get to
know it well. As one owner expressed it:

> *He suffered from a serious pancreatic deficiency, so it was*
> *necessary to observe him closely in order to keep him stabilised.*
> *We became very close through close observation of each other.*

From the dog's point of view, suffering or stress may
increase its attachment to a constantly present owner. It is
now thought that the physiological effect of pain or stress
on the brain facilitates bonding: animals who are shy of
people may become tame after being exposed to people
while in this state. For example, one scientific paper
reports the case of a wild Soay sheep who became tame
after a difficult birth. She needed human help and evenu-
tally a Caesarian section. Thereafter, when she had recovered, she would follow people around.

In addition, some people derive a great deal of satisfaction from nursing a damaged dog back to health. Sometimes, this damage is psychological rather than physical. One owner wrote of her black Labrador, her favourite dog:

> *As a rescue, initially shy of strangers and terrified of traffic. After re-socialisation, devoted to me and the rest of the family. I had had to work very hard to boost confidence and to train her, but the end result was a well balanced and devoted bitch. Mentally, there was something between us which I have not experienced with other dogs.*

To those who have experienced this satisfaction, the idea that others may feel the opposite may seem strange, but some people are repelled by the idea of owning a dog who is less than perfect. Mr M in Chapter 1, who had his Pekingese Mung destroyed rather than give him a female hormone, is an example. People who get satisfaction from 'repairing' dogs may feel that this needs no explanation; after all, they are on the side of the angels. Although it is true that this kind of attitude, directed towards all kinds of objects (ill people, Rumanian orphans, endangered elephants) is responsible for a great deal of good in the world, it still requires some explanation, if only because, as we shall see later in this chapter, it can sometimes have unfortunate results.

The urge to repair damaged people or animals is based on an internal scenario which involves damaged people, either ourselves or others. This feeling, often deeply buried, that we have hurt someone or been hurt ourselves, is as universal a phenomenon as needing love and comfort. If a baby is kept waiting for something, for a feed or to be picked up, for example, his normal reaction is to get very angry with his mother. You can see small babies in this situation getting purple and beside themselves with rage. At this age, it is impossible for the baby to distinguish between a feeling and an action: when he gets angry with his mother, he feels as if he is actually attacking her. (Even as adults, we feel guilty when we think nasty thoughts about someone, as if these thoughts by themselves could harm the person.) The result is that we carry these imagined attacks on our mothers through life in the form of a 'dead albatross' scenario: there is a damaged, disabled person in our internal world. People are dominated by this scenario to different degrees. Its importance can be increased if real events seem to confirm it: illness or disability in ourselves or our parents, for example. A good example of this is the owner of Bones. She clearly has a dominant rescue/repair scenario. Not only is she drawn to an extremely damaged dog, but her dream is a 'rescue' dream:

> *No idea where I was or what I was doing but my dog was in water and not able to get out and being slowly swept away. I got a long branch and tried to reach out to him – it wasn't a river yet there was a current and too deep to get into. I can't remember what actually came next but I suddenly could reach him and hauled him out by the scruff of the neck – I woke up. Once, when I was about fourteen, I was alerted by a dog's barking. I knew there was something wrong and went in search. I found the dog at the side of a straight-sided pond barking and another dog in the pond, unable to get out. I got it out and they both ran off – the dream could have been a throw-back to that almost forgotten episode.*

One reason for the recurrence of this theme is obviously her father:

> *Outgoing, cheerful, very popular with all age-groups. Dogs all loved him. A bad case of MS, paralysed for about thirty years – yet all the dogs we had would go and sit or lie beside his wheelchair. He could talk to them but couldn't move his hands to touch them. They all understood. My relationship with him was very good – despite the MS he was a super father and fun to be with.*

Here is a dearly loved, but damaged father. His daughter must have wanted desperately to make him better, partly because she felt (as all children do feel) obscurely responsible for his condition. She dreams about and remembers with such emotion the rescue of the drowning dog, because this is a parallel situation – but this time she can do something about it. She could not rescue her father from his multiple sclerosis, but she could rescue the dog from drowning. In the same way, later in life, she is able to rescue Bones.

As I mentioned earlier, repairing damaged people or animals is a constructive way of responding to them – much better than feeling hopeless and leaving them to their fate or even attacking them. It is more accurate to say that people who get satisfaction from repairing others do not have dead albatrosses but wounded albatrosses in their scenarios – albatrosses which have something going for them and are capable of being nursed back to health. So it is significant that the owner of Bones had a good relationship with her father and she perceived him as having positive attributes: 'outgoing, cheerful, popular' – he was damaged, not destroyed. Those who, like Mr M, cannot tolerate a damaged or imperfect dog have more badly damaged people in their scenarios, people damaged beyond hope of repair, so that all that one can do is push them out of sight.

> Another owner who completed my questionnaire is also clearly grappling with issues of damage, through her dogs. She does not ignore the damage, but does not feel able to repair it, either. She is a secretary in her thirties, living alone with several dogs. She has difficulty in walking, because of a riding accident in her teens. She has a good relationship with her parents, but says that her mother has battled against ill-health most of her life. Her relationship with her father is 'often stormy – we are very alike. For example, if we are doing a DIY job together (he helps me with a lot of my DIY chores at my house) he will get irritated because I perhaps see a way of doing

something quicker than him. I then get irritated because he seems to be doing everything the long way around.'

Her dog dream is of an Irish Setter: 'She is somehow on the roof of a office block recently built opposite my parents' house. I see her there and try to call her to get her to come down (I think there was a way down the back of the building, but I was being idiotic and calling her from the front). As I call her, she jumps off the roof (three storeys high). I wake very upset just as she hits the ground.' About the dream, she comments, 'If you can make sense of the dream perhaps you could let me know. I can't. Maybe it is to do with the fact that my Irish Setter has just been diagnosed as having lymphosarcoma. She is, or was until she was ill, a very lively and outgoing dog and pretty impetuous at times. I can imagine that she might just be silly enough, if she got very wound up, to jump off a precipice. I have been very unlucky with the health of my dogs. Indeed, I have only managed to keep one dog in double figures so far over the last twenty years. It seems very unfair, as I love and look after my dogs, I believe, better than many people.'

She indicates, then, that her dream is to do with a feeling that her dogs are blighted with illness. There are strong hints that she feels that this blight stretches back into her past. For example, the office block from which the Irish Setter jumps is near her parents' house. Also, in her Kelly grid (Figure 6) her mother and all the dogs (all blighted by illness) are fairly close together; in particular, her mother is seen as identical to the Irish Setter. She also indicates in the dream what she unconsciously feels to be a reason for this blight. The Irish Setter jumps partly because she is an impetuous dog, but partly because the owner herself has rashly invited her to take this shortcut. She feels that a similar wish to take shortcuts makes her relationship with her father stormy. It seems that she feels that it is this impatient part of her character which has done the damage.

In the Kelly grid she sees her 'ideal self' as being bold and self-confident, like her mother and her dogs. (I wonder whether she feels her rashness also caused her riding accident.) In reality, however, she sees herself as lacking in self-confidence. It seems she feels unsure of herself because she cannot trust her impetuous, 'idiotic'

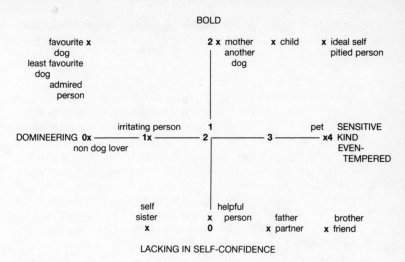

Figure 6

part not to pop out and wreck things. It is this which makes her feel so hopeless about her dogs and their illnesses. If she felt less intimidated by this part of her which she feels to be so damaging, she might feel better about her dogs: rather than, 'However hard I try, my dogs die on me,' she might be able to feel, 'My dogs have a better life with me than they would with most owners.' After all, the average life expectancy of a dog is around four years.

The trouble about being a dog repairer is that, in order to give satisfaction, the dog must get better. Dogs who don't do this can be a sad disappointment. A community mental health worker of her least favourite dog, a basset:

I loved her, but she also had a chronic skin problem and from birth presented us with continual visits to the vet. Her skin problem meant she was permanently on cortisone and she scratched incessantly: hence the dilemma of looking after her when she was not well really ever.

More common than chronic physical problems are chronic behavioural problems. Many 'least favourite dogs' had become alienated from their owners because of their behaviour problems. The more severe of these were often seen in rescue dogs, for example:

> *I took this dog on for Beardie Aid for assessment and he was with me for a year. I decided quite quickly that we could not safely re-home him, but he could have remained with me given significant improvement. Sadly this never materialised. He would respond to commands only if the other dogs did so. Alone he looked at me blankly. He could be exercised safely off lead away from the sound of traffic and came to me with the other dogs but not when he was alone. He became an increasing disruption with my other dogs with redirected aggression and sadly after twelve months he was put down. I still feel guilty about him but we subsequently discovered that he had been hit by a car at an early stage and frankly I suspect residual brain damage. To compound matters his pedigree was a disaster of nervous, over-excitable, aggressive dogs appearing on both sides of the line.*

This owner seems to have handled the situation well. She tried to treat the dog's problem and gave him a good chance of a home with her, but when he showed no signs of improvement she did not allow the situation to drag on and impair the quality of life of her other dogs. However, some people take on rescue dogs without any kind of realistic idea of what is involved. They may feel, for example, that their good deed consists merely in giving a poor, homeless dog a home. As a consequence, it will be grateful and will therefore be particularly good and loving. The reality is that rescue dogs are probably more likely to suffer from behaviour problems than dogs acquired as puppies. There are two reasons for this. Firstly, a behaviour problem is often the reason why an owner feels alienated from a dog and wants to get rid of it. Secondly, the experience of being passed from home to home seems itself to produce problems. An American study has shown that problems of destructiveness in the owner's absence are more common in rescue dogs. This is probably because, like children away from home in foster care, they feel insecure. They are therefore more likely to be agitated when their owners go out and leave them.

Miss M, a technician working at the Veterinary School, came to consult me about her little mongrel, Mimi. She had got her from the Dog and Cat Home a month before. When she was at home, Mimi followed her around everywhere, which she found gratifying. But if she was out of the flat for any length of time, she would come back to find paintwork scraped, furniture chewed and puddles on the floor. She would then become very upset and angry with Mimi, and would shout at her and hit her until she hid behind the sofa. Miss M was not at all a suitable owner for Mimi. Her work meant that she was forced to leave Mimi for hours at a time and when she did return, she would increase Mimi's level of stress still further by punishing her. Even when it was explained to her, she was unable to accept that Mimi's destructiveness was not directed at her – Mimi was not being ungrateful or spiteful – she simply could not stand the stress of being left alone. Since Miss M could not accept this first premise, all my suggestions – that she stop punishing Mimi when she came home, that she stop giving Mimi fierce lectures about behaving herself before she went out, that she try to find someone to look after Mimi for part of the day at least – were unacceptable to her. Nevertheless, she continued to haunt the clinic. The department where she worked was just across the courtyard and she would pop over at odd times looking for me to tell me tearfully how bad a dog Mimi was being and how she could not stand it any longer.

I knew that, before any progress could be made, I would have to explore with Miss M her feelings about Mimi: I suspected that she found unbearable the idea that Mimi's destructiveness arose from missing her and this was the reason she rejected it so forcibly. But this exploration would take time. It could not be conducted in five minutes in a corridor. But Miss M never turned up for any fixed appointments. It was as if she didn't want insight into herself or the problem: she just wanted the problem removed and that I could not do. In the end, she stopped looking for me. I never found out what happened to Mimi.

So if you take on a dog for repair, you should make sure that you have enough time, facilities and emotional energy to give yourself at least a chance of doing a good job. Furthermore, you must be prepared for the possibility that you will fail and be prepared either for living with that failure or for euthanasia. A few years ago, I saw an owner, Mrs R, who impressed me because she seemed to have come to terms with this so well.

> Mrs R had owned dogs all her life, but when she was widowed in her seventies, she decided to take on a 'last' dog, a rescue dog. She was unlucky, because he turned out to be a Cocker spaniel with so-called 'rage' syndrome. This is a tendency to attack suddenly and without warning, which must have some hereditary basis, as it occurs much more frequently in some breeds and most often in whole-colour Cockers. In my experience, this is a variant of dominance aggression: it is triggered off by what the dog perceives to be a challenge to his dominance status, in these cases usually being approached or touched on the hind quarters. It usually responds to the standard treatment for dominance aggression, but the outlook is not as good: because the dogs move so quickly from an ordinary, calm state to a state of ferocious aggression (often with a glazed look in the eye) it is difficult for a victim to avoid being bitten. This is what was happening to Mrs R. When I saw her, the situation was intolerable. Rory often attacked her in the kitchen, when she was preparing food. Sometimes, she had only to reach down a tin from the shelf – presumably it looked like a tin of dog food and he felt she was about to eat it – for him to jump up and bite her on the wrist. He slept on her bed and when she disturbed him in the night by turning over, he would bite her legs.
>
> I felt that the prognosis was not good, and that Mrs R, particularly in view of her age, deserved a better dog. But she said she had travelled a long way to see me, this was her 'last' dog and she was determined to have a go. In fact, she worked very hard at reforming Rory and he certainly did improve. His attacks were no longer a daily occurrence and (although this worried me) she said she could tolerate the occasional outburst.

But eventually a visitor who had not learned to read his body language was bitten. A friend was chatting to Mrs R in her sitting room and happened to touch Rory, who was sitting beside her, with her foot. He immediately bit her on the leg. Fortunately, she was wearing leather boots and was not hurt. But the incident convinced Mrs R that Rory was too dangerous and she had him destroyed. When she telephoned me to tell me of this outcome, I sympathised with her. She was sad, but philosophical. She said, 'I did the best I could for him and there are worse things than being dead.'

6 ● Dog as Lover

There are some dog–owner relationships in which describing the dog as parent, child or repair job is inadequate. The dog may be any or all of these things, but there is such passion, such emotional intensity in the relationship, that it is clear that something else is going on. For example, take these three women in their thirties:

> [Of a Dobermann bitch:] She is my soulmate, my precious, my best friend. I have plenty of human friends and a relationship with my boy friend whom I love, but nobody as much as her.

> The little Border collie I have at the moment means everything to me. I have an overwhelming love for her and any human being including my husband and son takes second place. I am sure the deep love I feel for my dog is abnormal. I had a dream which upset me terribly: a man stole her. I couldn't let her off the lead for weeks after in case anybody took her. I feel terrified when I think one day I will no longer have her. I feel I cannot cope with my feelings regarding how I will feel when she goes.

> My first Dobermann was Tommy. He was big and good-tempered. I won eight obedience trials with him. He died after my husband kicked him (he was standing in front of the TV). Then I had Thunder. He grew up very much my boy, my dearest love. My husband shows no affection to anyone: he largely ignored Thunder, so Thunder showed little interest in him. I could do absolutely anything for Thunder, teeth, ears, toe nails, etc. But he wouldn't relax to let anyone else even examine him – which is why I didn't show him. He was put to sleep in April – aged nearly thirteen. Now I have Tear-Away. He is my whole world. Unlike Thunder, he is everyone's friend and is Mum's

darling of course. We have done very well showing and he is
coming on in obedience. He knew it all at four months, but
enjoys playing me up and being naughty! He sleeps on the sofa
upside down, tummy exposed (see plate 1), so he obviously has
all the self-confidence in the world. Thunder always curled up
and tucked his nose in. If I had money of my own, I would get a
divorce and make a new life for me and Tear-Away. I am
contemplating it anyway.

More extensively documented is the relationship between
J. R. Ackerley and his Alsatian bitch, Queenie. Ackerley
was literary editor of the *Listener* in the 1940s and 1950s. A
homosexual when homosexuality was illegal, in his early
adult life he had a succession of lovers, all of whom turned
out to be unsatisfactory in the end. When he was almost
fifty he 'saw . . . that I was becoming what Guardsmen
called an "old pouff" . . . and that my chance of finding the
Ideal Friend was, like my hair, thinning and receding'. At
this point, Queenie entered his life. She was passed on to
him by a boyfriend, who could no longer look after her.

For the next fifteen years, his life revolved around
Queenie and she was devoted to him (see plate 2). He
wrote in 1949:

'Never a dull moment' I think to myself when I look back over
my four years with Queenie. What a rare thing to be able to say
of any relationship.

At this time, he was spending his lunch-hours queuing for
rationed meat for Queenie's delicate stomach. He would
carry it home in his rucksack, along with his papers, and
contributors to the *Listener* were sometimes alarmed when
their manuscripts were returned to them covered in blood-
stains.

She was certainly not the most well-behaved of dogs.
One of his friends wrote:

She acted quite wolf-like if one looked in – baring teeth, snarling,
raising ruff. . . . His method of discipline when discipline was

*called for was to smile at Queenie and say in a tone of intense
affection and delight, 'Queenie, I'll murder you.' Queenie would
wriggle with pleasure and wag her tail, and do just what she
wanted.*

Nevertheless, he took her with him to parties, where she
swept glasses and ornaments off tables with her tail, or
took up a position under a table where she growled at
those who tried to help themselves to food. She also
accompanied him when he went to stay with friends, but
she was sometimes less than welcome. Ackerley himself
rarely blamed Queenie for her bad behaviour, but was
aware that his friends were less forgiving. On a visit to
Siegfried Sassoon, Queenie made a mess in the bedroom.
Ackerley notes in his diary:

> *Queenie, I must praise her, such an intelligent dog, had
> deposited [the mess] on a dark mat . . . instead of on the
> beautiful thick white pile carpet which covers the floors of most of
> the rooms in the house. . . . I debated whether or not to tell S of
> this mishap. Was inclined to do so, then decided against; it
> seemed like sneaking on my dear doggie.*

As his love for Queenie deepened, so his sexual interests
faded away. He writes, again in his diary:

> *A great red lorry farts and groans among the trees at the edge of
> Siegfried's wood. Some workmen move about here putting chain
> and tackle round the trunk of a felled tree. I think to myself as I
> watch Queenie roaming about after a rabbit in vain, 'The c***s!
> They have frightened all the rabbits to earth; they are spoiling her
> sport!' Then I think to myself, 'Dear me! A few years ago when
> there was no Queenie you would have put down your books and
> strolled . . . up to that lorry to inspect the workmen.'*

Why do some people become so passionately attached to
their dogs? It often seems to happen when the owners are
lonely, human relationships having failed them. But such
intense attachments often attract criticism. Most of Acker-

ley's friends disapproved of Queenie, not only because she was such a nuisance, but because they felt he was making a fool of himself. E. M. Forster called her 'that unnecessary bitch'. People tend to disparage relationships or interests or hobbies when they can't empathise with the pleasure they bring, when they see only the trouble they cause. But, in some instances, the disapproval seems more intense: it seems to be based not so much on concern for the well-being of the participants as on a feeling that the relationship is morally improper. The reasons for this are explored later in this chapter. This condemnation can make people who love dogs intensely feel alienated from the rest of society, in the same way that other minority groups such as homosexuals feel alienated. In recent years, societies such as the Society for Companion Animal Studies have endowed dog-loving with greater respectability by collecting and encouraging scientific studies which demonstrate the benefits of owning a dog or indeed any other pet. And indeed there is plenty of evidence that, especially for people living alone, pet ownership tends to improve health and general well-being. I think this was probably true even of Miss S and Sweetie who could only eat fish or chicken and also of Miss H and Honey the anorexic dachshund. Certainly such a relationship can in some cases be life-saving.

> *A single woman in her fifties lost her parents in a fire. She writes, 'I turned to alcohol for comfort. I had been ill for some time and I was 22 stone in weight. I went to a clinic after some operations and the surgeon said, "Go out and get a dog, my dear, it's better than any prescription." I thought, "Silly man, what a daft suggestion," but the more I thought and wondered about his comment the more it appealed to me. I saw an advert in a newspaper and phoned. I got Ginger, my wonderful Cavalier King Charles. I dreaded it but he seemed to know I was awkward. I never looked back. We went everywhere together and everyone knew me as the woman with the wee Prince Charlie. I am now 12 stone and still trying, but not too hard, to cut down. I don't drink.'*

Some people argue that an intense relationship with a dog can be harmful, because it provides a false solution. An American psychologist, Leonard Simon, supports this argument with case examples such as that of a mother who neglects her family because she bestows all her love and concern on a kitten; also a husband and wife in an unsatisfactory marriage who become preoccupied with their dog rather than working at the relationship. I can see that this is theoretically possible but, in my experience, it rarely happens. People who become very involved with their dogs when their human relationships get sticky usually find it easy to drift away from the dog again once the human situation improves. In other words, the dog is a support, rather than a prison. Intense human relationships, taken up in times of stress, can be more problematic: for example, a husband who has an affair because of difficulties in his marriage may find that the relationship acquires a momentum of its own, which he had not bargained for. Most dogs accept philosophically the fluctuations in the intensity of their owner's affections, but some are less able to cope with them and develop problems. Prince in Chapter 11, who became aggressive towards his mistress's new husband, is one example. More common is the dog who develops separation anxiety, when his owner's new-found human interests take her out of the house. So it is the dog, rather than the owner, who is the potential casualty of an intense relationship. If you are the owner, you can prevent such a casualty by being aware of how you are using your dog and, when you become less involved with him, by letting him down gently.

Ackerley was an owner who rejoiced in the difference between dogs and people. He was well aware that Queenie and he often misunderstood each other and found great enjoyment in trying to puzzle out what she was trying to communicate. He noticed, for example, that dogs make each other's acquaintance by mutual sniffing of the ano-genital region. He made up some rude rhymes about this and he also consulted experts, such as the Director of London Zoo, on the subject. In this, he was unlike many intensely involved owners who feel that they and their dogs understand one another perfectly and even communicate telepathically. One respondent to my questionnaire claimed that she could 'think her dog upstairs in the morning'. A housewife in her thirties writes of her Rhodesian ridgeback (see plate 3):

> *I cannot describe the degree Livingstone and I are bonded: I have never had this bond before and doubt I ever will again. He is on the same wavelength as me mentally. It is as if he can stare at me and mentally tell me what he wants. All my other dogs have gone to the door and cried or scratched to go to the toilet. Livingstone can come up to me and look at me. I know whether he wants to go to the toilet, wants a drink or just wants a cuddle. I cannot describe how I know and now I have started thinking about it I must admit it frightens me a little. Am I going crazy? This telepathic bond between Livingstone and me also works the other way. I can be thinking of something – for example, having a bath – I will go upstairs to find him laid by the side of the bath. This is quite strange because our only WC and shower cubicle are in the bathroom: if I am going for a shower or to use the toilet he will stay downstairs. Occasionally I go to bed to read, leaving the boys and my husband watching TV. I will go upstairs and he will be waiting by the side of the bed.*

Understanding someone and being understood in this way can be immensely reassuring. It is the opposite of being lonely. It has its roots early in life, before a child has words, or even gestures, to express his needs and feelings. He relies on his mother to appreciate them intuitively. When she does, he feels secure: it is almost as if he and she were one person. When she doesn't, he feels utterly abandoned and alone. When a child learns to speak, he can communicate his needs much more easily, even to those who are less finely tuned to understand them. But communicating via words does not produce the same feeling of security as being understood without them.

However, when you feel you understand someone instinctively, there is a temptation to assume that they are the same as you, that they share all your feelings and wishes. With dogs, as with people, this can lead to problems.

Ms T and her St Bernard, Trudi, were a striking sight in the clinic waiting room. Ms T matched Trudi well, being of Wagnerian proportions and wearing a calf-length brown cardigan. As Ms T rose to greet me, she apologised for her lateness in a loud, clear voice, saying it was due to a heavy period. This announcement caused a brief, startled silence in the waiting room. Once in my consulting room, Ms T described the problem. Trudi's difficulties were due to disordered female hormones, she said. Although Trudi had been spayed, around the time when she should have been coming into season, in September, she started to behave bizarrely. She would follow Ms T and her children around the house, panting. She would jump onto wardrobes and chests of drawers and sit there panting. She would wake them up in the middle of the night by pacing up and down or holding her face close to theirs and panting. To me, this did not sound so much like a bitch in season as a bitch under stress. It was now April and the behaviour had not improved; in fact it had got worse. Also, when I went into things, it turned out that in September there had been various crises in Ms T's life. She was admitted to hospital with 'hormonal problems'. (In contrast to her announcement in the waiting room, she was now rather reticent about these.) She had also given a lot of money to a man to invest in a venture in the Edinburgh Festival. The venture had failed and the man had disappeared. Normally a freelance journalist, she had been forced to take up paid work in an office. A month or two later, they were also compelled, because of lack of money, to leave their flat in the centre of Edinburgh and rent a furnished flat in the suburbs. Trudi then became even more disturbed. The owners of the flat had African connections and it was filled with African carvings and masks. Ms T felt these exuded some kind of malign force: strange sounds were heard in the night and the children insisted on sleeping with the light on. Ms T was sure that Trudi sensed this too as her nocturnal pacings and pantings became much worse.

Ms T said she was interested in supernatural phenomena generally. She felt that she and Trudi were so close that they could communicate with one another via ESP and dreams. While they were still living in their own flat, she dreamt that Trudi had jumped out of the window and been killed. As a result, she kept nagging the children to make sure the windows were closed. But, one day, as she came home, she saw a group of tourists gazing up at her window. In spite of her nagging, the window had been left open, but on the window-sill of the thick-walled Edinburgh house Trudi was sitting, quite unflustered by all the attention she was attracting.

It seemed to me that Trudi was being disturbed, not by hormones or African ju-jus, but by Ms T's own behaviour. Ms T said that in the last few months she had felt at the end of her tether much of the time. While she sometimes felt very worried about Trudi, at other times she lost her temper with her. For a dog who was obviously bonded closely with Ms T this must have been very stressful. Then there was the added strain of being left alone in the house during the day, when previously Trudi had been accustomed to Ms T's company all the time. It seemed to me that the most likely explanation of the prophetic dream was that for some time before Trudi climbed out on the window sill Ms T had noticed (without being consciously aware of it) that Trudi was showing interest in the window and that there was potential danger there. Her dream had performed the useful function of reminding her of that fact. Because Ms T felt that Trudi was a kind of twin soul, she could not see that Trudi's perspective on the situation was quite different from hers. She attributed to Trudi her own hormonal troubles and her worries about the supernatural.

But she was an intelligent woman and interested in new ideas. She was intrigued by my explanation and was eager to try out my suggestions: that she try to behave consistently and rather coolly towards Trudi, neither being too cross nor too loving; that she try to ignore Trudi's odd behaviour (insofar as it is possible to ignore a St Bernard panting in your face) but to pay attention to Trudi when

she was behaving normally. On her next visit, Ms T
reported a great improvement. I was rather irritated by
her attributing this to the fact that they had moved out of
the spooky African flat rather than to my
recommendations; but perhaps it would have been too
much to expect that overnight Ms T abandon her
attachment to the supernatural.

When two individuals have an intense emotional relationship, outside observers often wonder whether sex is
involved. Ackerley's friends certainly wondered. Olivia
Manning, who wrote *The Balkan Trilogy*, asked him straight
out. He replied ambiguously, 'Only a little finger work.'
There are certainly sexual overtones in many dog–owner
relationships, even if the owner is unaware of it. The
owner of Thunder quoted earlier in this chapter is an
example of this. An even clearer example is the Hon. Mrs D
M and her Dandie Dinmont C in a coffee-table book with
glossy pictures of English stately homes, their dogs and
their owners. Of them, the authors write:

> C enjoys languorous nights on the bed of his mistress. . . . 'He
> always sleeps on his back, exposing his three-piece suite.
> Imagine, he was a rather dull, unattractive puppy and it actually
> took me a year to fall totally in love with him. I fell in love with
> his eyes and that huge black nose. I adore his big fat paws.
> Divine, naughty C you are so beautiful.'

Or the married woman in her forties who writes:

> Have had dreams about dogs which become sexual. Dog turns
> into a male human. Has never got as far as intercourse!

But actual sex between dog and owner is rare. According to
Kinsey, who finds startlingly high frequencies of most
sexual activities, 8% of men and 3.6% of women have sex
with some kind of animal. He suggests that the idea of
women having intercourse with animals is more interest-

ing to men than it is to women, which accounts for its recurrence in legend (e.g. Leda and the swan) and in pornographic material. However, where dogs are concerned, his data suggest that more women than men are involved: 2.6% of his sample of women had a sexual experience with a dog, whereas there was virtually no sexual contact between men and dogs. It seems likely that even Ackerley was only teasing his nosey friends. In his autobiography he wrote (and as elsewhere in the book he is almost embarrassingly honest about his sexual behaviour, there is no reason to disbelieve him):

> *In truth, her love and beauty when I kissed her, as I often did, sometimes stirred me physically; but although I had to cope with her own sexual life and the frustrations I imposed upon it . . . the thought of attempting to console her myself never seriously entered my head.*

More interesting than the question of whether owners do or don't have sex with their dogs is the question of why it is illegal and the idea is so shocking. After all, if coercion or sadism is not involved, it seems a harmless activity. A few centuries ago, people felt even more strongly about it. In 1679, a woman and her dog were hanged at Tyburn for bestiality. People's reactions to another dog–owner relationship of the same period shed some more light on the matter. Prince Rupert, a nephew of Charles I, went to fight in Europe in the Thirty Years War at the age of thirteen. At nineteen, he was captured and imprisoned for three years in the castle at Linz with only his poodle, Boy, for company. On his release he returned to England to help with the command of the Royalist forces in the Civil War. He was a reserved and difficult man but, understandably, very attached to Boy, who accompanied him everywhere. He was responsible for the Royalist army's initial successes (Boy even accompanied him into battle) and he became the target of Parliament's propaganda machine. Their pamphlets dwelt at length on his relationship with Boy. For example:

> I have . . . had a strict eye upon Prince Rupert's Dogge called Boy: whom I cannot conclude to be a very downright Devill, as is supposed . . . but certainly he is some Lapland Lady, who by nature was once a handsome white woman, and now by Art is become an handsome white Dogge, and hath vowed to follow the Prince to preserve him from mischiefe.
>
> He salutes and kisses the Prince, as close as any Christian woman would; and the Prince salutes and kisseth him back again as favorily, as he would any Court-Lady, and is as little offended with his Breathing. Then they lye perpetually in one bed, sometimes the Prince upon the Dog, and sometimes the Dog upon the Prince; and what this may in time produce, none but the close Committee can tell.
>
> . . . I beseech you now consider, that this Dog was once a Woman, but is now a Profane Metamorphosis Dog . . . that he is as shot free as if his skin were voted Impenetrable; that he can be invisible when he wil; insomuch that he is often smelt where he is not seen; that he communicates with that bloody Prince as his familiar; that he loves Organs, and tune singing and such Diabolicall Charms . . . it is impossible to destroy him, untill the Colonies of new England come in to help us; they know how to order these Dog-Witches better far than We.

Boy survived the battle of Edgehill, but was killed at Marston Moor (see plate 4). This caused wild rejoicing by the Parliamentarians and triumphant verses were published:

> Lament poor Cavaliers, cry, howl and yelp
> For the great losse of your Malignant Whelp

And, for whatever reason, the Royalist fortunes did start to decline thereafter.

It seems that at that time a close relationship with an animal, especially a sexual relationship, was connected in people's minds with witchcraft and black magic (see plate 5). This idea persists even now: people dressed as animals and engaging in sexual activities often feature in accounts of satanic rituals. Why should sex with animals be seen as devilish? One possible reason is that the point of some satanic rituals, for example saying the Lord's Prayer backwards or going 'widdershins' (counter-clockwise) round a church, seems to be that they violate the established order of things. Another name for the Devil is the 'Lord of Misrule'. Sex with animals violates the natural order because it crosses the species boundary. Secondly, many satanic rituals mix sexual and excretory functions. Witches were supposed to pay their respects to the Devil with an 'osculum obscenum': kissing the Devil's anus. As we will see in more detail in Chapter 10, the sexual behaviour of dogs is upsetting to some people, both because it is so blatant and immodest and because courtship in dogs involves sniffing at one another's urine and anal gland secretions.

An even more unsettling way of getting close to another individual is eating him. I am not suggesting that British dog-owners serve their pets for dinner, but the idea does appear in fantasy. One owner wrote of her Rottweiler, 'I love him so much I could eat him.' This feeling may seem odd when expressed about a large, presumably rather tough and gristly dog, but doting grannies do voice the same sentiments about chubby baby grandchildren. People in other parts of the world do actually eat dogs. The much publicised eating of dogs in Far Eastern countries such as the Philippines seems to have nothing to do with getting close to them, but merely to do with taste in food. However, the Sioux Indians both loved their dogs and ate them. When the nineteenth-century explorer, George Catlin, visited them, they honoured him by killing a large number of dogs and making a special stew. Although it was 'well flavoured and palatable' he had difficulty in eating it. He writes:

> The Indian will sacrifice his faithful follower to seal a sacred
> pledge of friendship. . . . . I have seen the master take from the

bowl the head of his victim and talk of its former affection and fidelity with tears in his eyes.

It is interesting that the reason for the taboo against eating dogs is the exact opposite to the reason for the taboo against having sex with them. We feel we mustn't eat dogs because it would be like cannibalism, i.e. like eating our own species.

All these bizarre activities are worth mentioning, not because people actually engage in them – they rarely do – but because fantasies about them lurk in our minds and colour our attitudes. The fantasies about dogs and sex in particular often fuel disapproval of too close and intimate a relationship between dog and owner. For example, this seems to be the best explanation of the vehemence with which some experts insist that dogs be kept out of bedrooms; and the resulting shame and guilt of some owners when they confess that this is where their dogs do sleep.

7 ● *Dog as Slave*

I have written in Chapter 1 how surprised we were to fall so in love with our first dog Mhairi. Another thing I had not anticipated was how much trouble she would be. For one thing I was used to a cat's ability to house-train himself: show a kitten a flower-bed or a litter tray and usually he will instinctively know what it's for. Mhairi made puddles everywhere. And she wanted intense emotional inter-action all the time. I had known some very sociable cats, but even they had their own business to attend to for part of the day. As I mentioned in Chapter 1, one of the embarrassing manifestations of Mhairi's passion for human company was her habit of rushing up to any stranger – in a shop, in the street, in the park – and greeting them enthusiastically. It belatedly occurred to me that there was a thing called training you were supposed to do with dogs. This led to the second surprise: Mhairi seemed so easy to 'train'. I don't know quite what we did, but, in no time at all, she was coming when we called her, sitting when we said 'sit' and staying when we said 'stay' – usually. It was almost as if it was a relief to her to get some instructions at last, as if she had been wondering all the time what we wanted her to do. (But we never managed to cure her of her habit of trying to share the sandwiches of people on park benches.)

Mhairi's daughter, Kirsty, was quite different. She co-operated in sit-stay training sessions, but looked bewil-dered and seemed to have forgotten it ten minutes later. She also got worked up very easily into over-excited states.

Before a walk she ran round and round in circles yapping so that it was difficult to put her lead on. Once in the car, she ricochetted from window to window, still yapping. This reached a crescendo when the car stopped outside the park gates and for the few yards between car and letting her off the lead inside the park it was like wrestling with a thing possessed.

I know now that my experience is shared by many dog owners, but at the time I was disconcerted and baffled. My first thought was that, if training had solved my problem with Mhairi, then the answer to Kirsty's problem must be yet more training. I went to the Public Library and was heartened to see a shelf full of books with such titles as *Training the Family Dog*. But, when I read them, they consisted mostly of what seemed like instructions for military drills, starting with sentences such as 'Commence the exercise with the dog at your left side and hold the lead in your right hand, which should be about waist-height about the centre of the body.' Judging by the illustrations, this sometimes was meant to result in almost acrobatic contortions (see plate 6). It all seemed to have little relevance to my problem with Kirsty.

Soon afterwards I caught mumps from my daughter. During this illness I found myself having some rather peculiar and light-headed thoughts. One of these was that what dogs who behaved in inconvenient ways required was psychological treatment, not 'training'. After all, many of the treatment techniques used in clinical psychology, particularly behaviour therapy, were originally based on experiments with animals.

These struck me as fascinating insights at the time and they still seemed interesting when I recovered. When I looked into it, I discovered that other psychologists had been thinking on the same lines and that a few papers had been published. That was what started me off as an animal psychologist.

Much later, I went back to the shelf of training books in

the library. I wanted to puzzle out who read them and why. Some of the readers probably had ambitions to compete in obedience trials, but this could not account entirely for their well-thumbed and much-borrowed state. By now I knew that it is not as easy to teach some dogs to obey simple commands as it had been to teach Mhairi. Some dogs have such a strong drive to be the dominant one in the family hierarchy that it can be difficult to persuade them to accept a subordinate role and take orders. But I also knew that if a dog will not obey simple commands, the answer is not to teach him more complicated ones. The whole pattern of interaction between dog and owner over the entire day needs to be restructured (see *Problem Dog*).

The right ending to this story would be, of course, that with the application of psychological treatment techniques Kirsty became a model dog. Unfortunately, it didn't quite happen like that. Kirsty settled down, but only gradually, with age. The only difference that animal psychology made to her was that seeing the range of things which dogs can get up to made me bother less about Kirsty's behaviour.

The more I read of these training books, the stronger grew the impression that most of their readers could not take them seriously. For example, most of them have chapters on how to train dogs to attack 'criminals', complete with photographs of men with guns being set upon by ferocious Alsatians. These would be worrying if the instructions were not so complicated.

It struck me that these books are like the catalogues for 'survival' equipment, illustrated with photographs of rugged men in the Himalayas and used by people who go no further than the local nature trail. What the readers of the books and the catalogues really want is the atmosphere and the fantasy – and the atmosphere and fantasies of many of the training books are rather disturbing. One of the prototypes of these books is one by a Colonel Konrad Most. Though first published in 1910, it has been regularly reprinted up to 1984. Here is an extract:

Secondary inducements, for use at a distance, are in the first place accents, ranging from gently admonitory to loudly menacing, words of command, including an intimidating sound such as 'Bah!' and in the second place our bodily attitudes and movements, graded from threatening to an actual attack upon the dog. . . . Implements to be used in the case of primary compulsive inducements are the collar, the choke collar and the spiked collar, in combination with the lead. There is also the switch, which can and should be used with a lightning flick of the wrist. . . . In conjunction with the lead, the collar not only serves to cause discomfort but simultaneously to draw the dog to the trainer's left side. In the down exercises a flick with the switch inflicts discomfort and simultaneously causes the dog to drop down in an instant.

Clearly, as time went on, the publishers began to get cold feet about some of this and in the 1984 edition they add a footnote to warn against the use of the spiked collar, 'except in the case of an exceptionally difficult dog and in the hands of experienced trainers'. And, in books written more recently, the sadism and the compulsion are not so nakedly expressed. But in the books of the gurus of the eighties, such as Barbara Woodhouse, the Prussian army flavour still lingers:

I teach the handlers in my class to do this exercise in a long line, with their dogs at the end of the lead facing them. . . . I give the command 'Now' and handlers give their dogs the same command as my next. Should I say 'Down', the handlers must raise their right hands and bring them sharply to the ground with the command 'Down'; the dogs must drop instantly to this position.

The central fantasy of these books seems to be that of completely controlling another individual. However liberal-minded and permissive we consider ourselves to be, we can all feel the appeal of this fantasy. When I was a child, my grandmother had two dachshunds. I remember little else about them except the excitement of being allowed to take them for a walk round the block on their leads. The reason why this was so thrilling was that I was in complete charge of what they did. This intense pleasure in being in control of their pets can often be seen in children. They will often play with their hamsters or gerbils by allowing them to run a little way, then blocking them and forcing them to go in another direction. This can make watching adults uneasy (though not as uneasy as watching a child 'cuddle' a gerbil) because the child seems to be teasing the animal. For the child the driving motivation is to be in control.

This feels particularly important to children because they are in control of so much less of their lives than are adults. And the same is even more true of a baby: physically helpless and dependent on his mother, he cannot even control whether she stays with him or leaves him to cry. So whether we can control the behaviour of others is an important issue for all of us early in our lives. For some of us, it stays important and for some dog owners it is the primary satisfaction in the relationship.

> *She was quick to learn and became the most obedient dog I've ever had. Bold and almost fearless – would try anything if I asked her to. (A Border collie.)*

> *When he runs one eye is always on me . . . When I got him from the rescue he was a total head-case but now he looks to me as pack leader and will do anything for me. (Irish Setter.)*

Conversely, for some owners, disobedience is what makes a dog the least favourite:

> *Since she was four months old, she has become a force in her own right. She took off into the shrubbery and totally ignored me, chasing rabbits, voles etc. I've increased my dominance over her and have noticed a slight improvement, but suddenly she'll take off. I had a loan of a shock collar, but the day it was returned her attitude was 'Great that's gone, now I can get on with hunting.'*

For others, disobedient dogs are the stuff of nightmare:

> *Very often I dream that my dogs are out of control and I am*
> *trying to get them on leads and haven't got any.*

So what makes the issue of control so important to some owners? A good deal of research has been done into areas related to this. Before going any further, readers might like to try the following questionnaire:

For each of the following statements, say whether you: (a) strongly agree; (b) moderately agree; (c) slightly agree; (d) slightly disagree; (e) moderately disagree; (f) strongly disagree.

1. Patriotism and loyalty are the first and most important requirements of a good citizen.
2. Foreign refugees may be in need, but it would be a mistake to relax our immigration quotas and allow them to flood the country.
3. Every person should have deep faith in some supernatural force higher than himself to which he gives total allegiance and whose decisions he does not question.
4. Young people sometimes get rebellious ideas, but as they grow up they ought to get over them and settle down.
5. When a person has a problem or worry, it is best for him not to think about it, but to keep busy with more cheerful things.
6. Most people don't realise how much our lives are controlled by plots hatched in secret by politicians.
7. No weakness or difficulty can hold us back if we have enough will-power.
8. The wild sex-life of the old Greeks and Romans was tame compared to some of the goings-on in this country, even in places where people might least expect it.

To find your total score for the questionnaire, first score each item as follows: (a): 7; (b): 6; (c): 5; (d): 3; (e): 2; (f): 1.

Then find the sum of the scores on all eight items.

If the wording of some of the items seems slightly peculiar, it is because they are taken from a questionnaire devised over forty years ago (although it is still used today). In the aftermath of the Second World War and the Holocaust, psychologists were keen to investigate whether there was a certain kind of personality which predisposes people to become prejudiced against minority groups such as the Jews and to support a Fascist or Nazi type of regime. From the results of questionnaires, interviews and other tests, they formulated the concept of the 'authoritarian personality'. According to this theory, a person with an authoritarian personality tends to see human relationships in hierarchical terms, with leaders giving orders and followers obeying them (items 3 and 4). They gain a feeling of security by being loyal to an in-group (item 1) and are hostile to outsiders (item 2). They find having conflicts or mixed feelings about something difficult to cope with (item 5): they deal with these conflicts by projecting unpleasant or sexual motives onto other people (items 6 and 8); also by seeing themselves as powerful and tough and denying any feelings of weakness or inadequacy (item 7).

Authoritarianism is a dimension, with the majority of the population clustered in the middle and fewer at the extremes. On the mini-questionnaire above, between 24 and 40 is an average score: two-thirds of the population score in this range. Above 40 is an authoritarian score and below 24 is a non-authoritarian score: only a sixth of the population score in either of these ranges.

The researchers also found that people with authoritarian personalities tended to have had a different kind of upbringing than the non-authoritarians: the authoritarians saw their fathers as strict and remote and their mothers as submissive and self-sacrificing. They felt that both parents demanded obedience to a rigid moral code. Non-authoritarians felt both their parents were more warm and approachable and that the relationship between them was more equal. They also felt their parents understood their point of view and gave reasons for the rules they imposed.

It seems likely that controlling their dogs is particularly

important to people with authoritarian personalities. It has been found that people scoring high on authoritarianism tend to prefer dogs to cats, presumably because you can't hope for obedience from a cat.

To a non-authoritarian, it might seem that being owned by an authoritarian owner must be a bleak and worrying experience for a dog. In fact most dogs seem to thrive on it. This is because wolf and dog packs are hierarchical organisations with leaders and subordinates. Most dogs are born with the instinctive behaviour patterns of dominance and submission: they are on the look-out for social cues as to which role they should adopt. On the other hand, rather like people, some dogs seem more preoccupied with their position in the hierarchy than others. Genetic factors play a part in this: guarding breeds and terriers tend to be more authoritarian dogs than spaniels or setters; hormones make male dogs and spayed bitches more authoritarian. And, as with the authoritarian personality in people, the whole tendency to view life in terms of power structures is present, not just the urge to possess that power.

So authoritarian dogs (like Mhairi) who see themselves as subordinate to their owners are more enthusiastic in their obedience than non-authoritarian dogs (like Kirsty) who simply don't see the point. Authoritarian owners are often understood best by authoritarian dogs. Dogs whose owners have allowed them to become dominant in the household are often under stress. They feel their position carries onerous responsibilities: protecting the family, deciding which visitors are safe to allow in the house and so on. They usually feel, too, that their dominant position is being constantly challenged by their unruly subordinates, their owners, who interfere with important tasks like chasing away the postman.

Authoritarian dogs are therefore often happiest when in a position subordinate to an authoritarian owner; this occasionally comes as a revelation to the owner:

Mrs F used to loathe her 'favourite dog', Fred. 'He had two hats – "More than my job's worth" and "Don't touch me, mate".' Before he was a year old he had bitten four people and threatened many more. One of these was 'the local Forest Ranger, dressed as an Easter bunny. Fred discovered him on a log within his woodland territory and proceeded to encircle him. In his consternation he fell off his log, to the children's delight and was only rescued by a properly dressed Forest Ranger and myself.'

The turning point came on a visit to the vet: Fred hated these and on this occasion 'he slammed me so hard with his body as I tried to get him in that I went flying. I was compelled to ask the vet to help. Fred turned his challenge on him too as I took him out of the car, but the vet's expertise put him firmly in control. Having dealt with the dog, he then dealt with the real problem. He blasted me out of existence: if I was beneath the dog, he shoved me into the abyss, then said, "Are you going to stay there or climb out?" I climbed out. I read every book I could, did a canine studies course and regained the assertive self I had before four children crushed it. I now have a lovely dog. Being one to earnestly search the Scriptures for the past two years, I found an added and most interesting experience gained from this incident: a recognition of the Edenic dialogue between myself and the vet in the car park. I had without doubt assumed the role of Eve by allowing one of the lower creation to dominate me.'

Mrs F has a classic authoritarian personality. Her Kelly grid (Figure 7) shows that she sees the world in one-dimensional terms, the dimension being the ability (or otherwise) to dominate people. Her father was 'hard and dominant, unaffectionate, unbending. Victorian disciplinarian'. Her mother was 'strong and very organising of people's lives'. Her parents are both at the dominant end of the grid, along with Fred. In spite of the confidence which she claims being able to manage Fred has given her, on the grid she is still very much the subordinate.

Although an owner interested in control usually has a satisfactory relationship with his dog, there can be pitfalls. In all kinds of species which live in dominance hierarchies

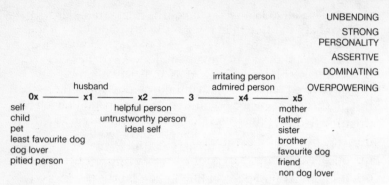

Figure 7

(e.g. monkeys, hens) it is the dominant individuals which initiate the most social interactions and respond to the fewest. Maintaining a dominant relationship over a dominant dog involves not responding to his requests or approaches (e.g. to be patted, to be let out, to be played with) and using the things he wants to reward obedience to your commands. Maintaining dominance is also a matter of bluff. You can't force a dog – especially a large one – to do what you want, but if he gets into the habit of obeying your commands, it will not occur to him that he has any alternative. This means not giving him a command in a situation where there is little chance of his obeying you: for example, when he is a dot on the horizon chasing a bitch. Expert dog handlers usually put these principles into action. But often they do it without thinking and could not put the principles into words; they have often been brought up with dogs and have learnt these techniques as one learns to talk – without being taught. When they write books on dog training, they don't spell out these principles because they can't. Instead they concentrate on specific concrete procedures such as training the dog to sit, always feeding him after your own meals or not allowing him in the bedroom. Their books are like the sex manuals which imply that if you adopt certain positions and do certain things your sex-life will be marvellous – ignoring the fact that the relationship between you and your partner is the crucial factor.

When first-time dog owners, who lack the instincts of the experts, read these books and put them into practice, they usually manage to gain adequate control of their dogs. But if the owner is very authoritarian, things can come unstuck, especially if the dog is very dominant too. If the dog doesn't obey a command, the authoritarian owner gets upset, because being in control is so important to him. He often blames the dog – maybe shouts and gets angry with him. The non-authoritarian finds it easier to maintain a degree of detachment and to try to work out what went wrong. Getting angry with the dog can have various undesirable consequences. For one thing, shouting a command to a dog while he is acting to the contrary is likely to teach him to act to the contrary, especially if obeying the command involves coming closer to be shouted at louder.

Mr and Mrs S consulted me about their Dobermann, Sultan. The problem was that when let off the lead in the park he tended to roam around, chasing joggers and barking at people in pink shell suits. He had never hurt anyone, but he frightened people and unpleasant scenes resulted. He paid no attention to calls from Mr or Mrs S and it was often difficult to get him back on the lead at the end of a walk. His behaviour was much worse with Mr S, who, it turned out, would become beside himself with rage on these occasions, screaming at Sultan and hitting him when he finally got hold of him. Mrs S could see that this was counter-productive, but couldn't work out what positive action to take. I explained to them how to establish general dominance over Sultan; I also suggested that they take him to the park at quiet times and keep calling him to them for a reward: Mr S was on no account to shout at him.

When they came back to see me a few weeks later, they said there had been only one episode of chasing, when a man had appeared suddenly from behind a hedge. But it turned out that this success had been achieved because Mr

S had refused to take Sultan out. The idea of rewarding and not getting angry with a delinquent dog went against the grain. He harked back to a previous dog who had come to heel at a click of his fingers: that was how a dog should behave and he would not be seen out with a dog who behaved differently.

Authoritarians often assume that getting angry with or showing aggression towards a dog is a very dominant action. In fact, what it signals to the dog is that the normal social conventions have broken down – aggression is not part of the body language of dominance and submission. The results are very much the same as when a fight starts between two people: the emotional temperature of the situation shoots up immediately. Behaviour also becomes less predictable: even nervous, submissive dogs or people may respond to aggression with aggression. A dominant dog (or person) is even more likely to respond to aggression by attacking. This can lead to a disastrous spiral of violence. For example an authoritarian owner tells a dominant dog to get off the sofa. The dog growls *sotto voce* and doesn't move. The owner hits him and shouts the order again. The dog bites him. It may not take many repetitions of this incident to convince the owner that he has a dangerous dog on his hands which must be destroyed.

Also the stress induced by aggression and punishment can aggravate behaviour problems which are caused by stress or anxiety in the first place. Not many people punish dogs with phobias (e.g. of thunder or of crowded streets) because it is usually obvious that the dog is afraid and cannot help it. But because they are intolerant of fear or any kind of weakness in themselves or anyone else, they may push the dog into the feared situation too precipitately, 'to show him there's nothing to be afraid of'. This tends to make the fear worse. Extreme fear can only be cured by introducing the feared situation very gradually, at a pace which the dog can cope with (see *Problem Dog*).

Authoritarians (and others) are more tempted to get angry with over-excited dogs, like Kirsty. This usually makes matters worse, as raising the emotional temperature just makes them more fussed and excited. Most potentially disastrous are situations where the dog is being destructive or messing in the owner's absence. As we have seen in Chapter 4, this is almost always due to the stress of being separated from the owner. Punishment is not only useless, because it is too far removed from the action in time, it is again counter-productive, because it raises the dog's general level of stress. Authoritarian owners are particularly likely to get into difficulty with this kind of problem. Their dogs are more likely to develop it in the first place, especially at night, because authoritarians feel everyone must be in their proper place and a dog's proper place certainly isn't the bedroom. Then, because they do not like to think too much about feelings, they are less likely to realise what the problem is. They are likely to construe the dog's behaviour as defiance and to punish him more the more he does it. And when they are told, by someone like me, what the problem really is, they are likely to react moralistically: dogs 'ought' to be able to tolerate being on their own.

Although there are still plenty of authoritarian owners, their views – or at least the extreme form of them – are not so 'politically correct' in the dog world as they once were. J. R. Ackerley was definitely a non-authoritarian owner: he wanted to understand rather than dominate Queenie. As a consequence, they had a very happy relationship, but he could not stop her threatening strangers:

> *It was when anyone approached her, or even gave the impression of being about to approach her, that she spoke her mind. She spoke sharply and loud, and had a good deal to say, though what precisely her mind was I did not know. In truth, although I was very anxious to know, I was less anxious to find out. Her sweetness and gentleness to myself were such that it was almost impossible for me to believe that these were not the prevailing*

characteristics of her nature; but the language she used to others certainly sounded pretty strong, and bad language, as is well known, does not always stop at that.

In his attitude towards dogs, Ackerley felt himself very much in the minority. This was in the 1940s and the Colonel Most school of thought still clearly held sway. In *My Dog Tulip*, he recounts his efforts to find an understanding vet:

It was a measure of my naivety in dog affairs that my first consultation with a vet was to enquire whether she was in heat. The question was never settled, that is to say by him, for when he was finally able to make himself heard, in his bleak surgery, above her deafening challenge and my own vain exhortations to her to calm herself, all he said, in a cold voice, was, 'Have you any control over your dog?' In the face of the evidence it seemed idle to return anything but 'No'; to which, still keeping his distance, he drily replied, 'Then take her out of my surgery at once.'

Some weeks later she sustained a small cut in one of her pads, which took so long to heal that I began to fear that it would never heal at all; another vet had been recommended to me, and I decided to try my luck with him. He was an ex-army man, a Major and the most I asked of Tulip on this occasion was she should allow me to flex her paw so that, without touching her, he could glance at the cut. But she would not permit even that. Having failed, as I had failed, to humour her or shout her down, the Major suddenly lost his temper, and exclaiming, 'These Alsatians, they're all the same!' he swooped upon her and beat her about the body with his bare hands.

These dashing military tactics were not without effect; they drove her, trembling with astonishment and fear, beneath his operating table, from the shelter of which she looked out at him with an expression which I might secretly excuse but could not approve; but they did not enable him to examine her, if that was part of his plan, and they could hardly be construed as an invitation to call again. They implied also, I took it, a rebuke to myself, as well as the more obvious one they meted out to her; they were teaching me a much-needed lesson in how to discipline an unruly dog: 'Spare the rod and spoil the child,' was what the Major was, in effect, saying.

Ackerley did eventually find a vet who correctly diagnosed the problem as protective aggression and who managed to handle Tulip without fuss by sending her owner out of the room. But vets like this were obviously few and far between. Forty years later, when British vets started to take seriously the scientific study of dog behaviour, there were still plenty of vets like the Major around. When I began, in the mid-1980s, to give talks to vets on the treatment of dog behaviour problems, there were always a few of them at the back, who, as I was speaking, would go progressively redder in the face and shift about in their chairs. When I had finished, they would get up to say that they had always smacked dominant dogs on the nose and would continue to do so. But now, six or seven years on, those red faces are no longer there. They have been replaced by faces wearing expressions of respectful interest. My subject has become accepted and respectable. The Majors have now turned their scorn onto activities such as dog homeopathy and dog physiotherapy.

A shift in the same direction has taken place in the dog training world. There are still plenty of authoritarian trainers around, using harsh methods, but there are now also many who use a more dog-centred approach, developing methods based on observation and understanding of dog behaviour. However that has come about, one happy result of this trend is that dog trainers and dog psychologists are now no longer automatically at daggers drawn, but have come to see that each has a lot to learn from the other.

8 ● *The More the Merrier?*

When new owners get a dog for the first time, and are very taken by the experience, they are often tempted to get a second dog, on the grounds that having two dogs must be twice as nice. It may not work out like that, exactly. Two dogs tend to form a mini-pack. However attached they are to their owners, they understand each other's body language much better than any owner can. A dog who has a tendency to yappiness may become more yappy if he has company, companionably barking at anything like adolescents giggling at non-existent jokes. If he tends to pull on the lead, he may become impossible to control when taken out with a friend: two dogs tend to twine their leads round their owners as if round a maypole. If the dog is of an aggressive, snappy breed – terriers are particularly bad for this – then the two dogs may end up fighting. This is especially likely if the dogs are of the same sex and if they are the same age and size.

In spite of these disadvantages, some owners go on to acquire a third dog, even a fourth or fifth. In fact, the more dogs you have, the more difficult it seems to resist the temptation to get another one. A second dog makes a big difference to the household; the addition of a seventh is hardly noticeable. But problems multiply with the number of dogs and owners of dogs in quantity do at times feel the whole business getting on top of them. For example, a lollipop-lady writes:

I have nine dogs, far too many for me to manage as I am now 64.
This weekend I have ten, looking after one of my previous pups,
whose owner goes away at weekends often. I have three dogs and
six bitches and it is unmanageable when the bitches are in
season. So about the eighth day of the season I take them up to
my friend's farm who has kennels. I am saving up to have the
four unspayed ones spayed. I haven't had a holiday for nine years
and I really need one! Being a softy by nature, I cannot find it in
my heart to rehome them: this wouldn't be fair to the golden
oldies, but I really should like to get down to two. It would make
life much easier from the point of view of exercising, feeding,
vet's fees etc. and keeping my home in much better condition.
What worries me is what will happen to them if I become ill.

The point about the condition of the homes of multiple
dogs is an interesting one. The standard of what is
acceptable tends to vary according to the number of dogs
the visitor has (see plate 7). The doggy smell, the number
of hairs on the furniture and the general level of dog
restlessness, barking and leaping up, in a four-dog household may make another four-dog owner feel comfortably at
home; but it may seem sluttish to the one-dog owner and
quite repellent to someone who has no dogs at all. Those
who have some insight into how their visitors might feel
can protect them to some extent. A nurse writes:

The first five dogs were excellent and the cats (five or six of them)
would mix freely with them. I have had more trouble with the
last three dogs who, although not aggressive towards them, will
not leave the cats alone if they come in the lounge. Therefore, it
has evolved that the lounge is the dogs' territory, my bedroom is
the cats', and the areas in between are mainly cats' but also
communal. There is one room I recently changed into an animal-
free people room for when friends come round who don't relish
being jumped upon by over-enthusiastic dogs and all covered in
hair.

So why do people keep packs of dogs? Broadly speaking,
there are two kinds of multiple owners: the 'Noah's Ark'
and the 'competitor'. To the Noah's Ark owners, their dogs

are their family. They either live alone or, sometimes, share their family with one other human partner. To them, this animal family is the most important thing in the world. Other people outside this charmed circle are much less significant.

For Noah's Ark owners, their dogs usually make up for human relationships which are denied them. For gay or lesbian couples or infertile heterosexual couples a dog family may be a substitute for children. Or the dogs may provide an emotional outlet for those trapped in unsatisfactory human relationships:

> *I think I give and receive all my love for my dogs. My daughter and I have a great deal in common and we really get on well, but her home is 600 miles away in London. My sons are fine lads but they have their own homes and partners and I don't share much of their lives. My husband expects me to LOVE, HONOUR AND OBEY.*

Or for those who, often in later life, have lost friends or relatives. The lollipop-lady in her sixties previously lived in Greece. She writes:

> *I have led an interesting life and have had a lot of boy friends and travelled a lot and speak three languages fluently. But now I am without relatives: no husband, no parents, no sister.*

But some prefer an animal family, finding human relationships too problematic. Indeed, the animals often help to keep the humans at bay. The nurse with ten cats, eight dogs and a good deal of insight writes:

> *My mother has the knack of making me feel inadequate because I do not live up to her idea of the perfect daughter. I was a quiet, well-behaved, polite child who totally rebelled at adolescence and have remained what my mother calls 'eccentric' ever since. My values are different to hers in as much as my animals are more important to me than holidays, an immaculate house, better finances etc. She likes animals, but up to a point. She knows I*

1 Mum's darling: Tear-Away asleep on the sofa (see pages 82–3).

2 The love of his life: J. R. Ackerley and Queenie (see page 83).

3 Livingstone, the telepathic dog (see page 87).

4 The death of Prince Rupert's dog Boy at Marston Moor, from *A Dog's Elegy or Rupert's Tears*, 1644 (see page 92).

5 Dogs as witches' familiars, from *The Discovery of Witches*, 1647 (see page 93).

6 Dog training: Barbara Woodhouse 'putting a dog down' (see page 96).

7 Some people may find visits to the homes of multiple dogs disconcerting (see page 111).

"It's a little chilly, so I've put an extra dog on your bed."

8 A 'Noah's Ark' owner: Kate and her dogs collecting funds in Camberley, 1968 (see page 114).

9 An Edwardian dog show, from Judith Neville Lytton's *Toy Dogs*, 1911 (see page 114).

10 Whose sex life is it anyway? The recommended technique for mating large pedigree dogs (see page 117).

Cy deuise des alans et de toute
leur nature.

11 Alans were probably the medieval ancestors of the bull terrier (see page 133).

12 Goya's 'Sorcerers changing into dogs', 1797 (see page 134).

13a and **13b** Before and after rescue by the SSPCA (see page 157).

14 An American pit bull in its training gear: the dog had to pull against the weight of the concrete blocks (see page 166).

DOG FASHIONS FOR 1889.

Dorcupine, Crocodachshund, Pomme-de-Terrier (Black-and-Tan), Ventre-à-Terrier (Scotch), Hippopotamian Bulldog, German Sausage Dog, Hedge-dog, Bug-dog.   *(By Our Special Dog-fancier.)*

15 Exaggerated breed differences are not a new problem (see page 178).

*have ten cats, but thinks (as far as I know) that I have only four
dogs. She has thrown a wobbly at every animal, especially dogs,
I've had, so I gave up telling her. She never comes to my home
and I've made it clear that it's out of bounds.*

*Until recently, before undergoing psychotherapy, I was very
obese and scared of romantic/sexual relationships. The obesity
was my own 'suit of armour' to keep people away. In fact I
became very socially withdrawn, although I had friends and went
to work and functioned reasonably well. I've always been an
animal lover and I'm sure that even if I'd been the most stable,
emotionally healthy person in the world, I still would love them.
However, I do recognise that to have a complex houseful of them
is rather a pathological symptom of my inability to form
satisfactory relationships with the opposite sex.*

*Also, I do not get maternal feelings about children and have
never wanted babies, but put a puppy in my arms and the feeling
that wells up is almost overwhelming. Luckily (for them) I still
love them when they're adult and most of my animals have been
adults when I took them in.*

*Recently, I have lost over seven stone. My self-esteem has
risen, so I am hoping I may extend my affections to my own race
soon, if I can find a man worthy of them who likes animals! They
are rather a handicap when it comes to my social/romantic life
but it's definitely love me, love my dogs and cats!*

Most Noah's Ark owners feel a bit uneasy about the ever
increasing size of their menagerie. Many deal with this by
not taking active steps to add to their family, but they
passively accept animals which fate pushes their way. This
usually means rescue animals. The nurse again:

*Most of them were strays apart from Bisto, my first and
favourite, who I had from two young boys in the street. They had
been told to get rid of her and were asking passers-by. She was
nine months and in season, so presumably this was the reason. I
took her, meaning to rehome her, but I was frightened she would
be dumped on the street. It was mutual adoration! All the others,
except Nora, a collie cross, were strays off the streets. No
informing the police or advertising ever raised previous owners
and, apart from one (whose owners I met by chance two years
later) had probably been dumped. Most were distrustful and/or
nervous and thin and neglected.*

This way of acquiring dogs has two advantages. The owner can't be blamed – by herself or by anyone else – for taking on yet more animals. Also it reassures her that she has an important and useful role in life: without her the animals would have suffered or died. Some of these owners become professional rescuers, publicly setting themselves up as animal sanctuaries and soliciting funds as charities. Although many dogs and other animals owe their lives to such organisations, there can be drawbacks when they are run by Noah's Ark owners. Such owners may find it difficult to maintain a throughput of animals. Understandably, they may feel that euthanasia is unacceptable, but some may even find it difficult to pass their inmates on to new homes: somehow, the prospective owners are never quite right. If the owners have difficulty with human relationships, they may also find the business of fundraising hard to manage. Some Noah's Ark owners find effective ways of attracting support (see plate 8), but one shelter I know of is in constant difficulties, not because it lacks would-be supporters, but because it alienates them by constantly moaning at them and criticising and interfering with the jumble sales and exemption shows they put on for its benefit.

The other kind of multiple owner is the competitor. These owners use dogs as a means of achieving some kind of status in the outside world. This can be in racing, agility, obedience, or most commonly, in showing and breeding. The show world is a fascinating and addictive one, full of emotional turmoil. The show world a century ago was the same, as plate 9 shows. But the emotions are not so much those of Victorian melodrama as those of Elizabethan revenge tragedy, involving intrigue, assassination, incest (among the dogs) and the rise and fall of dynasties. Hints of these goings-on are to be found in the dog press as in the headline 'Leading Airedale is poisoned' in *Dog World*, September 1991, or in a paragraph in the same paper, October 1991:

It is disturbing to learn that the despicable practice of sending anonymous letters to judges – both before and after they judge – seems to be on the increase. . . . One lady judge, whose knowledge of her breed cannot be questioned, had received several unsigned letters which were obviously intended to persuade her to put down a very beautiful and highly successful winner. Happily, she had the strength of character to put it up because she felt it was the best on the day. Good for her!

I acquired more inside knowledge of one of these sagas as a result of breeding from our second Cavalier, Kirsty.

My friend, Mrs C, who is in the show world, persuaded another breeder, Mrs F, to allow me to use her dog, Phantastic. Mrs F, a minor figure in the Scottish show world, had been taken up by Mrs S, an English Cavalier queen, and had become a court favourite. As a mark of her favour Mrs S had given Mrs F Phantastic, a promising young puppy. At the time when he became the father of Kirsty's puppies, Phantastic was just at the beginning of his show career in Scotland. I took Kirsty along to Mrs F's house for her encounter with the crown prince. It was not pleasant. Mrs F looked under strain: she was pale and drawn and she chain-smoked. She was also irritable and not very welcoming. Kirsty did not improve matters. She was not the beauty Mrs F had clearly been expecting for Phantastic. Moreover, she flirted with him outrageously, leading him on then moving away at the crucial moment. When eventually he managed a tie, she screamed without pause for twenty minutes. Mrs F was not pleased, muttering that she hoped that this did not put Phantastic off bitches for life. We parted on strained terms.

Two months later, Kirsty gave birth to two puppies and thereafter Mrs C kept me informed about their father's doings. He did very well in Scottish shows. Mrs F quarrelled with Mrs S. Mrs S tried to reclaim Phantastic but Mrs F refused to part with him. It was common ground that no money had passed, but it was never quite clear whether Mrs S had given Mrs F the crucial item, his 'papers'. Mrs F also began to claim that Mrs S had neglected and maltreated Phantastic and therefore had no moral right to him. Mrs S mounted some dawn raids over the Border arriving at first light on Mrs F's doorstep demanding Phantastic. She was repelled by Mr F whose temper and inclination to violence came in handy on these occasions. At one of the few shows I visited, I saw Mrs F looking even more pale and tense, sitting on a box covered by a cloth. She was smoking and glancing nervously about her. When I asked Mrs C where Phantastic was, she drew me aside and whispered that he was in the box. Mrs F was determined to show him but was afraid that Mrs S or one of her agents might try to kidnap him.

Rather fittingly, Phantastic turned out to be a poisoned chalice. On several occasions, at the high point of a show, while being judged for Best of Breed, he bit the judge. He could not have done anything better calculated to cause maximum embarrassment. The result was that he was quietly retired from show business. I, too, got my come-uppance for having been dazzled by the bright lights of show business. The puppy of Kirsty's which I kept was ravishingly handsome, but when he was six months old he started to bite the children, suddenly and without warning.

What are the satisfactions of the show world? First of all there is the beauty contest aspect. There is the possibility of basking in the reflected glory of owning a champion, perfectly formed dog. If you have bred that dog yourself, the satisfaction is much greater: it is like the satisfaction of growing your own prize onion as opposed to finding a winning specimen in the greengrocer's.

Breeding has other rewards as well. In helping the bitch give birth to and rear her puppies, there is the vicarious maternal satisfaction of bringing new life into the world. The gratifications of the stud dog owner are less obvious. Pedigree dogs mate in a bizarre way. In the wolf, courting starts weeks before the she-wolf comes on heat. A pair-bond is formed, usually between two wolves of high rank in the pack. The pair mate repeatedly over the days when the she-wolf is in oestrous; this activity attracts a good deal of interest from the rest of the pack, who gather round them in an excited group. Dogs have been selectively bred to be less choosy about their partners and to be able to mate without weeks of courtship. In spite of this, if left to themselves, they behave very like wolves. A pair who live together do a good deal of courting: sniffing, playing and running around. They may mate many times when the bitch is in season. In contrast, a pair of pedigree dogs whose mating has been arranged are usually allowed only a brief and carefully controlled courtship. They are then expected to stand still and get on with it, with the bitch restrained and the dog often handled and physically manoeuvred into position (see plate 10). This procedure often seems more like artificial insemination (which the Kennel Club rules in this country do not permit) than anything else. There are some practical reasons for it. This fixed ritual ensures that the dog gets into the habit of mating with any bitch put before him in that situation, but is not so likely to molest bitches in the park. Also, having the bitch to stay with the dog for days at a time would be inconvenient for the dog's owners. There might also be disputes about whether, or with which dog, the mating had taken place. It is sometimes said that the dogs have to be restrained in case they should attack each other. This sounds to me more like a human fantasy about the nature of the relationship between men and women than a canine reality.

The fact is that this human interference with their dogs' copulation meets other psychological needs in the owners. For example, in a female owner of a stud dog, it may satisfy a wish to dominate and control a male's sexual behaviour; alternatively, she may identify with her dog and get the satisfaction of playing the male sexual role. For both owners of dog and bitch, another more complex need is often satisfied. As children, most of us grow up aware at some level of our parents' sexual relationship. This is reassuring, it means our parents love each other. But it also makes us jealous, it is something important and exciting from which we are excluded. Most children harbour the wish to barge in on and put a stop to their parents' sex. (Most couples observe that their young children have an uncanny knack of being able to do this in reality.) In these managed matings of their dogs, breeders are at last able to turn the tables on these internal parents: manipulating, watching and being in the thick of the exciting action, from which, as children, they were humiliatingly excluded. Ironically, the dogs concerned probably don't perceive it this way. They probably see their owners as lower-ranking members of the pack – bit-part actors gathering around the stars.

Although most breeders are competitors, some are Noah's Ark owners as well, filling their household with surplus or substandard puppies. The lollipop-lady writes of four of her dogs:

> *Daisy is beautifully bred, but hates shows so I can't show her often. . . . Polly is one of her puppies but is shy like her mum. Minnie and Emma are puppies of Polly that I haven't been able to sell, because their ears haven't gone up. Minnie especially has developed into a bit of a freak. She has the correct coat, but is Queen Anne fronted and too long. She was nearly exported to Holland as people thought she had all the correct attributes. Fortunately, this fell through, or my name would have been mud. She is a case of a pretty puppy turning into an ugly swan, but she is very loving and lovable.*

Unfortunately such concern for individual dogs militates against success in the show ring. To stand the best chance of winning, you have to own as many potential winners as you can accommodate. Losers take up valuable space. Having losers around the house may also harm a breeder's reputation: if she values it, she will get rid of 'shy' or Queen Anne fronted puppies to owners unconnected with the show world or even by euthanasia.

Breeders often say that they love the breed (rather than the individual dogs). They may offer the 'good of the breed' as justification for disposal of substandard dogs.

This justification would be more acceptable if many of them did not at the same time keep quiet about defects in their champions which are less obvious but more serious. Research by vets has shown that many of these defects have a hereditary component. Dogs suffering from them should therefore not be allowed to breed. This fact is now well-established and accepted for defects such as hip dysplasia. There are other defects, such as heart murmurs in Cavalier King Charles spaniels, which need further investigation. Some breed clubs see that this is in the best interest of future generations of dogs and welcome research studies, even raise money for them. Others discourage and obstruct researchers, not allowing them to examine their dogs or denying that a problem exists. For people who profess to love the breed, this is an odd way to behave.

Part III
Aspects of Hate

9 ● *Dangerous Dogs*

On 14 April 1989, an eleven-year-old girl, Kellie Lynch, was killed by two Rottweilers. This event was a spark which set alight enormous public concern about 'dangerous dogs'. The event itself assumed a symbolic significance: 'Rottweiler' entered the language as an adjective (as in 'Rottweiler tendencies') and politicians appeared in cartoons with Rottweiler bodies to denote their bullying combative style. Various factors kept it in the public spotlight for a while. Kellie's mother, who projected a compelling combination of prettiness, frailty and determination, mounted a campaign for the special control of Rottweilers. She said, 'I don't want all living Rottweilers put down. I want them neutered or spayed and muzzled when they are outside.' The *Daily Record*, a Scottish tabloid, took up the campaign, less interested in the finer points of methods of control, than in descriptions of the doings of 'devil dogs'.

After a while, the public excitement died down, although pro- and anti-dog pressure groups continued their trench warfare. More responsible Rottweiler organisations tried to improve the breed's image and reduce the number of delinquent Rottweilers by offering training schemes and instructions to owners. Less responsible Rottweiler owners devoted their energies to firing air-guns at the Lynches' windows, sending them hate mail and desecrating Kellie's grave.

Two years later, four-year-old Rucksana Khan was attacked by a pit bull terrier. The dog broke away from the pregnant woman who was walking it on a lead in a park. It severely injured the little girl, but she recovered. But this incident once more sparked off the dangerous dog furore. It also provided a convenient focus for that furore. Because pit bulls had been imported relatively recently, for the unpleasant and illegal purpose of dog fighting, their owners could command less support from dog owners in general than could owners of more mainstream breeds such as Rottweilers or Alsatians. The Home Secretary initially proposed that all pit bulls should be destroyed. Pit bull owners, of course, protested vigorously. Owners of lovable old pit bulls, family dogs who had never harmed anyone, made expeditions to Downing Street to plead for their dogs' lives. It became evident that this measure was so extreme that it would be likely to provoke too much sympathy for its victims. The eventual provisions of the Dangerous Dogs Act of November 1991 were similar to Mrs Lynch's suggestions about Rottweilers, although of course they did not apply to Rottweilers.

They required that owners of all types of dog specified by the Act (pit bull, Japanese tosa, fila brasiliero and dogo argentino) had to register them with the police, and comply with the exemption scheme by having them neutered, permanently marked with a microchip, tattooed, insured and kept in secure conditions. In public, the dog had to be muzzled, on a lead and under the control of someone at least sixteen years old. Any dog that had not received a certificate of exemption was to be destroyed. It became an offence to breed or sell the specified types of dog.

The views of some individuals give a flavour of the passions aroused by this issue. When a local newspaper mentioned that I was interested in people's feelings about dogs, I received the following letters:

> *Dear Dr O'Farrell, I am writing to inform you how much I detest dogs. I absolutely loathe the canine species for the following reasons:*

a. *They foul footways and parks thus presenting a mini obstacle course to passers-by. Dog's faeces have been proven to harbour parasites which can cause blindness – children are particularly at risk.*

b. *Large aggressive dogs instil a mixture of hatred and fear within me – unhealthy emotions at the best of times. I have a 4 year old daughter and fear for her safety.*

c. *I object to the way some playful brute attempts to leave its filthy paw marks over my trousers.*

d. *Drug dealers and other shady characters sometimes use fierce dogs to obstruct the law in exerting its authority.*

e. *I object to the noise of their barking, particularly at night.*

My observations suggest a trend whereby the size of a dog is in inverse proportion to the size of the owner's brain. The elimination of the larger breeds might lead to an improvement in intelligence levels.

Yours sincerely.

Hi Valerie.
STAFFORDSHIRE BULL TERRIOR – PLEASE READ.
I am a dog lover on having a mungrel for 21 years which sadly had to be put to sleep. Crying for weeks and near Christmas I went out and bought a Staffordshire Bull Terrior. When I took it home my dad loved it straight away: whom I may add has a slight fear from any kind of dog. My mum was a bit annoyed with me at first because of all the grief we have went through with animals. Anyway now Sue is one of the family. She is tempramental and goes huffy when you leave her but when with her she is more loving than anything I have ever seen. She would just about lick you to death.

I personaly would actualy try to hurt any person who hurt a dog. I can't blame any dog for anything I blame the tubes who own them. Leave the animals alone I think. Punish the owners please.

There were also two stories which were even more disturbing:

I and my husband had been out late of an evening and I did not let my dogs out in the garden as it was very late and there were cats giving each other a punch up and making a din which my dogs would have added to. I put them on the lead and went 5 mins walk alongside a park and then walked past an old empty factory. I looked around and saw no one so I let the two dogs loose and they went down an alley which was grass covered. I looked to my side and saw a man in a grey jogging suit running towards me with something silver like a knife in his hand. I was so scared I tried to speak and nothing came out my throat, as the man came nearer I froze. The two dogs had seen him and stood him off. I picked up Mini Minder (my mini pinscher pup) and called JC (my Dobermann) to heel, which he did immediately but he was still growling and defying the man to come any nearer. The man said, 'That dog is as good as dead.' In the early hours of that morning I was awakened by a howl and went down. JC wanted to go out the back and then started to convulse. We got him to the vet who kept him and put him on a drip. Two days later we brought him home. He had to have liquid every two hours around the clock and tablets. He had to go to the vets each night for an injection. One evening when we came home and opened the front door, which leads to the front room where the dogs sleep of a night, on the floor was kebab-type lamb and Mini picked it up. I screamed and took it off him. He was bad by the time we got back to the vet, with the meat, which the vet said was fox bait. Mini recovered but JC only lived two days. His liver and kidneys gave out and he died in a pool of blood. I held his head in my arms.

And a single, sixty-year-old woman, the owner of three German shepherds, whose letter and its style convey her sense of desperation:

The MP saying, 'We will compel them to destroy their dogs' made me plan: leave keys, payment and instructions with vet and look for a multi-storey car park – end of household. Then I cut myself off, broke dog bonding, now I can handle it, but poor dogs haven't got trained these last days. In fact really getting left out quite badly. Felt absolutely desolate, rejected when told no need to have these creatures, children's lives are more important.

A few owners of dangerous dogs have indeed committed suicide. For example *Dog World*, 9 August 1991, reports:

Six-year-old James Walmsley was bitten on the leg by a Rottweiler. Later in hospital he was said to be comfortable. But

*the woman owner involved and her dog were later found dead in
a fume filled car.*

Why does this issue generate so much public and private
emotion? Let's start with the arguments on both sides.
Although there are differences of opinion within both
camps, coherent versions of each point of view might run
as follows:

Anti-dog: All dogs are dangerous but some are more
dangerous than others. Ideally, people should not be
allowed to own dogs (except perhaps for a useful purpose
such as guiding the blind) or at least should not be allowed
to let them loose in public. Failing that, this should at least
apply to the more dangerous breeds.

Pro-dogs: Most dogs are gentle and friendly. The few
that are dangerous are made so by their wicked and
irresponsible owners, or are provoked by their victims
teasing them or behaving in some other silly way.

What are the facts of the matter? Fatal dog-bites, though
tragic, are very rare: there are only one or two per year in
Britain. (Horse riding accidents cause, on average, thirteen
deaths per year.) Non-serious bites, on the other hand, are
very common. One study has estimated that one million
people are bitten each year but only 17% of these seek
medical treatment. So it seems that most dogs are indeed
dangerous, but only mildly so.

And do victims of dogs provoke their attackers? The
details of the Kellie Lynch case are relevant here. From
newspaper accounts of these tragedies it is often difficult to
make out how the attacks happened, but in this case I gave
evidence at the fatal accident inquiry and so had direct
access to first-hand accounts.

Kellie went to spend a fortnight with a school-friend
whom I will call Susie. Susie's father was separated from
her mother and ran a hotel in Dunoon, a small Scottish
seaside town near the American nuclear base at Holy
Loch. His new wife's hobby was showing Rottweilers and

at that time they had two: Jody and Cassie, a two-year-old dog and bitch bought as puppies from Northern Ireland, complete with 'temperament certificates'. They were kept in an outdoor kennel and run, but were taken out regularly for walks. No evidence emerged of any aggression before the time of the attack. One old lady in the neighbourhood said she felt nervous of them, but this seemed to be because they were big and bouncy.

Witnesses said that in the few weeks before the attack the dogs seemed more excitable and thinner. During this time, Jody met the old lady when out for a walk, jumped up on her and knocked her over. There seemed to be two possible reasons for this change in their behaviour. One was that their main owner, Susie's stepmother, was away in hospital. The other was that six months previously Jody and Cassie had mated. None of the resulting puppies had survived – fortunately as it turned out. But the relevant implication here is that Cassie may well have been due to come into season again around this time. Bitches about to come into season tend to be more active and excitable – a mated pair even more so.

On their holiday, Kellie and Susie took Jody and Cassie for a walk every day. (It is clear, especially with hindsight, that to put two young girls in charge of two Rottweilers was a silly and irresponsible thing to do; but which of us has not done something silly and irresponsible at some time?) On the day of the attack the girls took their usual route beside a river. At one point there is a spit of shingle jutting into the river which they called 'the Island'. When they reached the Island, Kellie needed to urinate, so Susie took the leads of both dogs. Kellie went a few yards away and squatted down. Immediately, the dogs became very excited and, breaking free of Susie, bounded over to Kellie and started to lick her. Her reaction was to laugh and at this point they started to attack her, biting her throat. Susie pulled them, kicked them and then finally interposed herself between the dogs and Kellie: but the dogs just pushed her out of the way and went on attacking. So Susie ran back to the hotel for help. But by the time her father arrived, Kellie was dead. He laid a windcheater over Kellie's body. A few minutes later a woman from the hotel ran up and, assuming that Kellie had drowned, pulled back the windcheater. When she

saw Kellie's mutilated body, she screamed. The dogs
immediately attacked her. Fortunately Susie's father
brought them under control at once and no further harm
was done.

This tragedy is a striking example of an action by the victim
– laughing or screaming – which the dogs clearly perceived
as some kind of threat and which provoked them to attack,
but whose effects on the dogs only someone with special
knowledge or experience could have predicted. This seems
to be the case fairly often in dog attacks. In a study of 146
dog-bite victims treated by a plastic surgery unit, one third
of the adult victims and a half of the child victims (or their
parents) judged the attack to be unprovoked. However, in
many of these cases, the researchers were able to identify
the provocative action, for example bending over the dog,
waking it, invading its territory or playing with it till it
became over-excited. The pro-dog and the anti-dog lobby
each seem to be half right: victims do usually provoke their
attackers, but not intentionally or by actions which would
generally be regarded as provocative.

Are some breeds of dog more dangerous than others?
Rottweilers and pit bull terriers certainly share a characteristic which makes them particularly dangerous: before they
attack, they give very little warning in the way of threats or
growls. (Vets dread treating them for this reason.) In the
case of pit bulls, this is clearly an advantage in the fights for
which they are bred: they can take their opponents by
surprise. It also seems reasonable to infer that the guarding
breeds are relatively more dangerous. To do the job of
guarding, they have to be able to show some aggression. In
addition, the small terrier breeds tend to be dominant and
snappy.

However, considering the amount of emotion which the
issue generates, there is a dearth of hard evidence on the
subject. I have collected some data on the subject, although
it has some limitations. In the course of research into

effects of spaying on bitches, 300 owners of unspayed bitches were interviewed and asked about their pets' behaviour. I divided the 300 dogs into eight groups: Alsatians, Border collies, rough collies, Labradors, retrievers, terriers, spaniels and mongrels. (The groups were determined by the dogs that turned up in the study; there were not enough Dobermanns, for example, for a meaningful comparison.) The groups did not differ significantly in their frequency of aggression towards family members, but they did differ in the frequency of aggression towards strangers: Alsatians and terriers showed significantly more of this kind of aggression than any of the other groups. One limitation of this data is that it concerns only female dogs. However, it seems likely that differences between male dogs of these breeds would be, if anything, greater. A more serious limitation is that it did not include some of the breeds which people feel most strongly about.

The aggressiveness of a breed, however, is only one factor in determining how much damage that breed inflicts on the human population. It also depends, for example, on how prevalent the breed is and how careful the owners are to keep them out of trouble. In the plastic surgeons' survey of dog-bites referred to earlier, Staffordshire bull terriers and Jack Russells were responsible for the most attacks and together accounted for a quarter of them. Labradors, Alsatians and mongrels together accounted for another quarter. The proportions were similar for severe and less severe attacks.

One interesting fact emerging from these surveys is that terriers, particularly Jack Russells, are comparatively dangerous dogs. Like Rottweilers, terriers can be provoked to attack by movement or by high-pitched noises. For an adult, this can mean a nip on the ankle when answering the telephone, but for a baby lying on the floor, kicking or crying, the results can be much more serious. But in the public mind, these dogs do not feature as dangerous, as the following incident brought home to me:

A woman telephoned me to ask if I would help with her case. She sounded distraught. She told me the following story. Her two-month-old baby had been crying all day and in the evening, in desperation, she left him crying on the bed and went out to her car, where she fell asleep. Her husband was asleep in the sitting-room. He woke up to find the baby still crying; one of his legs was out of his baby-grow and one toe had been severed. Their four-month-old Jack Russell was running around in an excited state. They rushed the child to hospital where the wound was dressed. But the hospital staff would not allow the baby home because they said they suspected ritual abuse. When the parents said the dog had done it, they replied that it was too neat an amputation to have been done by a dog-bite. Also, they argued, the dog could not have taken the baby's leg out of the baby-grow. However, a few days later a policeman arrived and took away the dog as well.

I thought that, although I was only hearing the woman's side of it, her account sounded plausible. She had described the typical circumstances of a terrier attack and I thought that the sharp teeth of a terrier puppy would be quite capable of parting the poppers on a baby-grow and of severing a baby's toe. I told her this and suggested that her solicitor contact me. Unfortunately, I heard no more about it.

Another point which emerges from the data is that a strategy of banning certain breeds is not likely to have the direct effect of drastically reducing dog attacks. Even if it were feasible, banning Staffordshire bull terriers and Jack Russells would reduce dog attacks by only a quarter at most. To achieve any further reduction, Alsatians, Labradors and mongrels would have to be banned – obviously an unrealistic proposition.

Are owners responsible for their dogs' aggression? After a dog attack which hits the headlines, journalists often ring me up and ask me this question. I am not sure how to answer them. There is the fairly obvious point that, in a legal or moral sense, an owner who knew his dog was likely to attack is at fault if it does so.

Recently, a woman from Stirling, a vet's receptionist, sued her employer because his two West Highland white terriers bit her on the ankle as she was getting down from a chair she had been standing on. The wounds did not heal and two years later she had to have the leg amputated. Because it was decided that the owner must have known that his dogs were liable to bite, she was awarded damages.

It is also clear that dogs cannot be held morally responsible for their own acts of aggression. As they cannot think in abstract terms nor understand the concept of rules, they cannot have a concept of 'right' or 'wrong'. It is therefore inappropriate to think of euthanasia as a kind of retribution which a dangerous dog deserves. Its sole purpose must surely be the removal of the dog from society, to prevent it both from doing further harm and from passing on its genetic inheritance. Pro-dog pressure groups sometimes get muddled about this point as when, in August 1992, the RSPCA pressed the government to review the Dangerous Dogs Act. They said some pit bulls were being 'unfairly' destroyed because their owners did not want the bother and expense of meeting the requirements of the Act.

But it seems to me that the journalists who ring me up have in the back of their minds a much more interesting idea: that the owner may be expressing through the dog part of his own personality; that, whatever the cause of the dog's aggression, it is also the owner's aggression.

It is useful at this point to consider the whole matter from a historical perspective. Dogs have always been inclined to aggression and dog attacks have always been a problem. The Romans used the Molussus, a large dog with powerful jaws (said to be an ancestor of the Rottweiler), as a guard dog and in war. There are frequent references in classical literature to dogs turning on their masters. Vikings too were accompanied on their raids by mastiffs but at home these dogs obviously posed a problem. A large section of the Gragasse, a law book drawn up in the eleventh century, is concerned with the legal position of dogs. Some of its provisions deal with the problem of dangerous dogs in a realistic and logical way which today's British legislators might learn from. For example:

> *The law holds that no trust is to be put in a dog. He who possesses a savage dog shall fasten it to a stake in such a way that it shall not be able to reach men going in and coming out of a house . . . if a dog is tied up in a privy it must not be allowed to reach men going therein or sitting on the seat or stretching out for the wiping cloth. If anyone shall tie up a dog without due care or in any other way than has been set out above or it shall bite any freeman so that his skin turns red or blue or blood gushes out, the owner of the dog shall be fined three marcs.*

In the Middle Ages, a dog called the alan – probably an ancestor of the bull terrier – was popular (see plate 11). In the thirteenth century, Gaston de Foix writes:

> *Always alans are prickly and nasty-tempered and altogether giddier and madder than other kinds of hounds so that I have hardly found three that have been kind and well-intentioned . . . if one pricks on a course they will set off at a gallop and will run kine and sheep and goats and any other animals; and again men and dogs and I have seen alans that have killed their master.*

As well as being concerned about real dangerous dogs, people were worried about fantastical or supernatural dogs. In many parts of Europe there is a black phantom dog; in East Anglia he is called Black Shuck (from 'succa', Anglo-Saxon for Satan). He is as big as a calf with burning eyes and an unearthly howl. You should shut your eyes if you meet him, for meeting his gaze is fatal. In 1577 he visited a church in Bungay, near Norwich:

> *There came a great tempest of violent raine, lightning and thunder, the like whereof hath ben seldome seene. A dog of a black colour . . . or the divil in such a likeness . . . ran all along the body of the church with great swiftness and incredible haste among the people . . . passing between two parishioners kneeling in prayer, it wrung their necks and they died immediately. . . .*

> *[It gave another man] such a gripe on the back that there withal*
> *he was presently drawen togither and shrunk up as it were a*
> *piece of leather scorched in a hot fire.*

There was also the Wild Hunt, a pack of hounds which could be heard howling, usually at night. In Wales they are the Cwn Annwn or Dogs of Hell. They are usually heard on windy days and, paradoxically, the further away they are the louder their baying becomes. Although they travel as a pack by air, they are visible only when they appear singly on the ground. They are omens of death and their colour is significant: if a white dog appears near the home of a dying person, it means his soul is saved, but if the dog is black, he will be damned.

Then there is cynanthropy or lycanthropy, the belief that people can change themselves into dogs or wolves. When people did this, it was never for some useful purpose like finding car keys dropped on a walk or rounding up some sheep, but to do something unpleasant, sometimes sexual and usually violent. The ability to change oneself in this way was often one of the professional skills of a sorcerer or witch (see plate 12).

> The most recent example I have found is that of a Mr
> Richard, who died at Bourg-la-Reine in 1930. He was a
> farmer who had a sideline in witchcraft; people in the
> neighbourhood would pay him to put spells on those they
> had grudges against. He was also believed to go about at
> night in the shape of a wolf. On his death, there were
> found in his house, among other things, a head of a calf,
> dried salamanders and wax dolls with pins stuck in them.

It could be hard to prove that someone was a werewolf: evidence was needed to connect the person with the animal. At the trial of a witch burnt in the Auvergne in 1588, the following story was told:

> *A man met a friend returning from hunting, who told him he*
> *had been attacked by an enormous wolf. Fortunately he had*
> *fought it off with his knife and in the struggle had severed its*

right fore-paw. When he pulled the paw out of his bag, it changed into a woman's hand with a gold ring on one of the fingers. His companion was horrified to see that it was his wife's hand. He hurried home to find her slumped in front of the fire with her right arm hidden under her apron. When he challenged her she uncovered the bleeding stump and confessed that she had been a werewolf for several years.

Living in a different, more scientific culture, we can stand back from these beliefs and even offer rational explanations for them. Black Shucks were presumably feral dogs who would normally keep their distance from human beings, but would sometimes appear unexpectedly and startlingly. For communities which did not have scientific explanations to draw on, the connection made between these dogs and death was presumably an attempt to inject some meaning and predictability into a world where accident and illness occurred so often and so unexpectedly.

I myself once saw one of the Cwn Annwn, in the Prescelly mountains in Wales. I knew nothing about them at this time, but when we were climbing a ridge, with the wind whistling round us, my Welsh companion casually mentioned that he could hear them howling. I did not pay much attention as he was always bringing bits of Welsh folklore into the conversation, but I was a little disconcerted when, at the top of the ridge, we saw on the opposite slope what looked like a Dobermann without any visible owner. I was even more disconcerted when, having looked away for an instant, I looked back to find it had disappeared completely from the bare hillside. My friend was mildly triumphant, but matter-of-fact; it was as if I had been sceptical about the presence of some rare piece of wildlife in the countryside and he had found one. I am glad I did not know then about the sinister implications of a sighting and that a black dog carried an especially bad prognosis. Twenty years later, as far as I know, we are both still alive and well.

The explanation of werewolves must be a complex one. There are several kinds of reality basis for the belief. Firstly, there is evidence that in Europe and North America certain groups or cults with satanic associations would dress up in wolf skins when performing their sexual or murderous activities. Identifying with a ferocious animal helped them to throw off their inhibitions. Also, some people with rabies must have been terrifyingly mad and dog-like, as they tried to bite those nursing them. There is also the mental illness of lycanthropy where the patient imagines himself to be a dog or wolf. This is now rare, presumably because the general belief in werewolves has also died out. When this belief was prevalent, some people probably encouraged it for their own ends. Poachers probably pretended to be a Wild Hunt to keep people away from their activities. Sorcerers like Mr Richard would encourage any idea that they were werewolves, to enchance their professional reputations.

Whatever its basis in reality, a belief in werewolves would have psychological benefits for the believers. A community subject to attacks by a wolf (which would be almost impossible to track down) must have felt very helpless. The pressures to find werewolves must have been similar to those which led to the convictions of, say, the Birmingham Six.

It is interesting that werewolves seem to have been more prevalent than weredogs. This is surely because, as we have seen in preceding chapters, as well as being feared, dogs are very much loved in various ways. Wolves on the other hand are almost always seen as dangerous and ferocious in reality and in the folklore which surrounds them: it is easier to hate them unequivocally than it is to hate dogs. In more recent times, as a result of studies of wolves which have shown them capable of complex and subtle social interactions, there has been a tide of feeling in their favour. In countries such as Italy where there are still wild wolves, there are now moves to conserve them. In some people this has led to a mistakenly romantic view of wolves and sometimes a wish to keep them as pets. But a tame wolf is much more dangerous than a dog: it is more likely to mount dominance challenges, for example:

> According to Erich Klinghammer, who has studied wolf behaviour for many years, even experienced keepers are liable to be attacked by a tame wolf pack. Sometimes a wolf seems determined to force a confrontation or fight, especially if the person is ill or debilitated in some way. He recommends that if a worker is attacked by a wolf he should not scream unless help is at hand, because this tends to excite the wolf, nor, for the same reason, should he run. The most effective ways for a victim or rescuer to fight back are to choke the wolf by compressing its windpipe or cut off the supply of blood to its brain by grabbing the loose skin over the scruff of its neck and twisting. A person who has been knocked down by several wolves should fall into a foetal position and go limp and still. This applies equally to dog attacks and may be reassuring to people who, like me, cherish information about what one should do in all kinds of unlikely circumstances.

Moving on to eighteenth- and nineteenth-century Britain, we find controversies about dangerous dogs very similar to those of the present day. But one important difference was that, until 1902, rabies was endemic. This meant that the death rate from dog attacks was much higher than it is now: about 35 per year in the late nineteenth century. Nevertheless the views of the pro-dog and anti-dog camps have a familiar ring. In 1877, a year in which there were 79 deaths from rabies, someone signing himself 'Cave Canem' wrote to *The Times*:

> *I suppose that even the most unreasoning lover of animals would admit that it would be better to exterminate dogs than to allow the increase of hydrophobia.*

But, in 1885, the *Kennel Review* defined rabies as a 'peculiar madness that seizes on men and impels them to destroy dogs.'

In 1796 compulsory dog licences were introduced and

throughout the nineteenth century other measures were considered or tried out: confining dogs, muzzling them or requiring them to wear tags. None of this affected the incidence of rabies. The trouble was people were not sure how rabies was transmitted. They knew you could catch it by being bitten by a rabid dog, but they thought rabies could occur in dogs spontaneously. It was Pasteur, of course, who clarified the whole matter. When, in 1887, the British expressed an interest in inoculation on a large scale, he told them:

> You do not require it at all. I have proved that this is an infectious disease; all you have to do is establish a brief quarantine covering the incubation period, muzzle all your dogs and you will be free from it.

And that is more or less what happened.

The historian Harriet Ritvo, analysing these rabid dog scares, has suggested that people were really worried not about the dogs who wandered around unsupervised but about the kind of people who owned them – the working class. There was a good deal of social unrest during this period and the middle classes feared the kind of revolution which was taking place in other European countries. Could it be that the current concern about dangerous dogs is due to the same kind of uneasy awareness that some of those sections of the population have, during the 1980s and 1990s, become seriously alienated from society, with a resulting general increase in violence? Dangerous dogs may have become a symbol of this, like inner-city riots or joy-riders.

All through history, people have used dogs as embodiments of their fears of violent attack. Why should dogs be such an attractive focus for fears of this kind? The answer lies in the way that dogs attack – by using their mouth and teeth to tear and bite. As a dog is usually regarded (and regards itself) as part of the human family, a dog attack on a person almost seems a cannibalistic one. Stories of murderers who eat their victims have a horrible fascination for us: take for example the success of the book and film *The Silence of the Lambs*. This fascination stems from our very early experience as babies when we are instinctively pro-grammed to feed off another person, our mother. When the feeding process goes smoothly, with the baby's hunger being followed by a satisfying feed, his feelings are manageable and pleasurable. On the other hand, when things go wrong – as they inevitably do sometimes – for example, when a baby is kept waiting for a feed, or when the milk doesn't flow properly, then the baby can quickly be filled with rage and frustration. When he does feed, he may attack the breast greedily, biting and perhaps causing his mother pain. Alternatively, he may turn away from it, as if afraid of it. Studies of a person's deep and primitive fantasies – in patients undergoing psycho-analysis, for instance – suggest that the angry, biting baby at that moment hates the source of supply and wants to damage it, rather like kicking a coffee vending machine which does not deliver. He then fears he may have destroyed his mother ('Oh God I've done it now – I've broken the machine') or that she will retaliate in the same way (just as you would feel it was poetic justice if the kicked machine gave you an electric shock or sprayed you with boiling water). Every baby has this primitive anger towards his mother and these primitive fears of retaliation from her. A normal mother survives her baby's rages without getting too fussed, and these bad feelings are contained within the framework of a loving relationship. The baby learns that his hate is not too destructive and that it is possible to love and hate the same person. But, from time to time, in adult life – when we are subjected to exceptional stresses, for example – these frightening feelings of primitive hate are liable to well up in us. Because they feel so frightening and unmanageable, we tend to project these feelings onto something in the outside world. The advantage of this mental manoeuvre is that then we feel we can escape from the danger by taking practical steps. If we project the danger onto dogs, for example, we can avoid dogs we see in the street and we can agitate for legislation to curb their movements even further. People who choose dogs as projection objects tend not to have been brought up with dogs or to have lived with them on intimate terms. They feel free to hate them without the complication of loving them.

While some people project their own aggression into dogs and then hate or fear them, however, others identify closely with dogs and express their aggressive feelings through them. (The fantasy of the werewolf is a vivid expression of this polarisation.) One ghastly example of this appeared in an account, in the *Scotsman*, 14 August 1992, of atrocities in Serbian detention camps:

> One guard liked to take his two Dobermann dogs through the prison, a large warehouse, and threaten to have the dogs kill prisoners. . . . Instead, several prisoners would be taken outside where their throats were slit and their bodies were cut open so the dogs could eat their entrails. . . . When the dogs would not eat those, the heads were broken open and [the narrator] said he saw dogs eat prisoners' brains.

Another example of dogs being used as instruments of aggression is mentioned by my dog-hating correspondent: the 'drug-dealers and other shady characters who use dogs to obstruct and hinder the law'. With them could be classed those who use dogs like pit bulls for fighting. These sorts of people are a godsend to dog lovers: they can hold them responsible for all the trouble with dangerous dogs and distance themselves from them.

More uncomfortably near to home, however, are those who might be called 'King of the Jungle' owners. They like to own a magnificent animal which is capable of doing a great deal of harm, although it is never allowed to do so. Rottweiler owners feel they are unfairly criticised, but, at the risk of offending them again, I feel bound to point out that the potential danger posed by these dogs must be part of the pleasure. It must be significant that even the show dogs have names like 'Daredevil' or 'Oliver's Army' (Best in Show at a Northern Ireland show).

> A good example of this kind of owner is Bill, a friend of mine, who had always wanted a Rottweiler. When he and his wife Betty acquired Wallace they took him to training classes and felt they had him well under control, although, as he grew bigger, Betty's awareness that she would not be able to restrain him physically made her apprehensive. Soon after the fatal attack on Kellie Lynch, there was some difficulty with friends with young children, who refused to visit unless Wallace was shut away. Bill felt insulted by this suggestion and refused. Damage was done to some friendships as a result. Having only seen Wallace as a puppy, I then met him two years later at a Hogmanay party. He was indeed a handsome and majestic dog, who moved slowly and deliberately among the guests. When I happened to catch his eye by mistake, he growled very softly, which unsettled me rather. I asked Bill if he had any problems with him. He laughed and said Wallace was inclined to attack other male dogs. Because of his size, Wallace always appeared to be the guilty party and Bill had had to pay several vet's bills. I normally try not to give advice on behaviour in social situations, but this time I could not resist commenting that castration often helped inter-male aggression. Though laughing, Bill jumped up and hugged Wallace, saying that he couldn't possibly do anything like that to him.

There are also legitimate handlers (for example, police-men) of dogs trained to attack. Some of these people take a similar pleasure in their dogs' aggression as this poem from the British Police and Service Canine Association's magazine *Service Dog* shows:

SULTAN: A True Story

He came disgraced from wild welsh Wales to be a policeman's friend,
A girl, you see, had teased him, so he bit her rear end,

Now, it's down to training. 'Only bite when you are told.'
And whilst his handler's watching he'll behave as good as gold.

For thirteen weeks he stayed the course, the days were hard and long,
But he grew to love his handler and soon the bond was strong,
He listened to his trainer and he passed in every test,
He didn't tell the others but he knew he was the best.

Now Sultan was a Police dog, the best you've ever seen
And he could smell smells, where smells had never been,
Famous were the tales as could be told about dog's nose,
Like the day he scented razor that was used to rip up clothes.

When men attacked with bottles, one of milk and one of beer,
He answered to his master's call and showed he knew no fear,
He bit one in the stomach who fell back and hit his head,
The noise he made, as he went down, brought neighbours from their
* bed.*

The other one, in drunken rage, tried hitting handler hard,
But as he raised his bottle high he found his way was barred,
With hackles raised and lips drawn back, the message growled quite
* clear,*
'Take one more step, you've had it mate, you're getting much too
* near.'*

A pause before the tension broke then bottle hit Sultan's head,
But not before he'd jumped aside and bit a moving leg,
His handler's voice 'Leave – Now down, we've caught a nasty pair,
I suppose they'll say in court, we didn't fight quite fair.'

The needs met by 'Kings of the Jungle' can be subtle and
complex and their roots go back, as we have seen, into
early life. The owner of three Rottweilers writes:

> *People often ask me why I like Rotts: I don't know. I remember*
> *looking through a book of breeds of dog when I was about ten and*
> *there was a picture of a Rottweiler standing on a hill and I was*
> *always drawn to that picture. Then my husband and I decided on*
> *getting a dog. So we looked through breeds etc and the same*
> *thing happened again: there was a picture of a male Rott stood*
> *looking totally superior to everything else. Of course I kept being*
> *drawn back to that particular page. I don't have them for a*
> *macho image: I cringe at the thought of that. What I see in them*

is a totally beautiful dog, who is superior to other dogs and knows it. They are so alert and very proud. They are totally devoted and loyal, my male especially, although he is aggressive to other dogs.

She also writes:

Things between my mother and I have never been good. There was a time when my parents had separated and my mother started telling my dad I was having nightmares and crying for him all the time and I wasn't at all. I found out that she was always using me to her own advantage. When I wasn't being used in some form of emotional blackmail against my father, I was ignored. When I was 17 I left home to live with an aunt. My mother started on about how ungrateful I was after all she had done for me.

She also writes about a dream about a mongrel called Fiddle:

A dream filled mostly with guilt i.e. the dog is accusing me of not loving her. I got Fiddle when I was four years old. She grew up with me, played with me and my toys, looked ever so bored when I dressed her up in clothes! But she was brilliant and the perfect shoulder to cry on. When I was 16 she had a fit in my bedroom. My dad took her downstairs and got her a bowl of water. He was placing it down when she flew at him like something demented, then she suddenly realised who he was and stopped. The vet gave her tablets but the fits came randomly, usually two weekly and it petrified me every time. Then one night she took a fit (they always came about five in the morning and I always woke up knowing what was going to happen) but she was lying by the bedroom door and as I tried to open the door to get my dad, she went for me. I stood behind the door and screamed and screamed which brought my parents running. It was decided it would be best for Fiddle to be put to sleep. After she had gone I couldn't get to sleep without having the light on. I used to have terrible dreams about her attacking me, she would be walking round me and I would be stood just never knowing when she was going to go for me. She would be telling me I should have treated her better and then she'd go for me. I used to hate going to sleep. I even used to hate being alone in the house, expecting to see her at the top of the stairs, drooling and snarling. When she was alive, though, she was the most wonderful, beautifully natured dog, a total contrast to the Fiddle in the dreams.

I find it very hard to show my feelings, except with my dogs who I adore and make it quite obvious. But with people I find it very hard and then I think others probably feel I don't care because I don't show them otherwise.

What this owner is saying is that her feelings are now expressed in terms of dogs, because her feelings about people are so problematic, particularly her relationship with her mother. The primitive anger in this relationship is dramatised in her dreams about Fiddle. She feels it consists of guilt, reproaches and murderous attacks. In real life, she puts distance between herself and her mother to keep them both safe from this anger, but in her mind the problem still goes on. She herself finds it puzzling why Rottweilers are so attractive to her. I think that the reason is that she feels that they protect her from the murderous scenario which goes on inside her head. Only a Rottweiler, which is 'superior to all other dogs', is dangerous and powerful enough to protect her from this 'drooling and snarling' which is both Fiddle and her angry mother.

Then there are the 'Oh you are awful' owners. These are usually owners of small snappy dogs who, while deploring and wringing their hands at their dogs' aggression, do not seem to be doing all that they could to control it; in fact they seem to be getting some secret satisfaction from it. Miss W, from Chapter 4 who lived with her elderly mother and William the large Yorkshire terrier, is an example. I came to the conclusion that part of the reason why she never acted on any of my suggestions as to how she might deal with William's tendency to snap at her mother's feet was that, though she didn't like to admit it, she herself felt very irritated with her mother. It suited her that William did the granny-bashing – it saved her from the temptation of doing it herself.

However, perhaps the most dangerous kind of owner is the 'He only wants to play' kind. These have such a problem with aggression that they deny its existence in themselves or their nearest and dearest. Even when the dog is growling and baring his teeth, they can't believe he really would do anyone any harm.

> I saw a golden Cocker spaniel once owned by a couple with two pre-school children and a crawling baby. They had told me on the telephone that the problem was that he chewed the furniture when he was left on his own. But when I saw them, it turned out that he also growled at and threatened the children all the time. He was especially bad in the kitchen: he would growl and snap if they brushed against him or went near their mother or sources of food such as the fridge. He had actually bitten the two older children on several occasions. Somehow the parents had dismissed the bites as mistakes or flukes. I spent a very difficult half hour with this couple, explaining to them that their dog was a great danger to their children, that it was only a matter of time before one of them was badly bitten. I had to say to them that, in their family situation, the problem was untreatable and the dog would have to be destroyed.

So, the anti-dog lobby and some owners have one thing in common: they both need dangerous dogs; the one needs to hate them and the other needs to love them. Does it matter? From a dispassionate point of view one might argue that hate and aggression are part of human nature and that expressing these emotions through dogs is a lot less dangerous than expressing them by means of guns or even fast cars. But from the point of view of the dog lover, dangerous dogs are a bad thing. Apart from the damage – both physical and psychological – to the victim, it also puts the dog at risk. Looking at past records of dogs seen at the Edinburgh University Small Animal Clinic, of those who had a diagnosis of aggression, before behavioural treatment became available in 1982, one third were eventually destroyed. It gives dogs in general a bad press and plays into the hands of the anti-dog lobby.

As an owner, there are some things you can do to avoid having a dangerous dog. To begin with, you can avoid the breeds liable to aggression – the guarding breeds and the terriers. Also, male dogs are more likely to develop problems of aggression than are bitches. Because there is a hereditary factor in aggression, you should try to find out as much as you can about your prospective dog's mother, father and siblings. If he does start to show signs of aggression, you should take it seriously and take behavioural steps to control it (see *Problem Dog*). You should also ask yourself whether you are wholehearted in your desire to stop it, because if you don't really mean business, you are much less likely to be successful.

> Mrs B consulted me about Betty, her West Highland White terrier, who spent her spare time pouncing and scrabbling at the floor as if there were small animals there. Although this behaviour seemed crazy to Mrs B, it is actually no more crazy than other more common stereotypies, like sexually mounting a cushion or digging in the flower beds. As we have seen, these are often caused by stress, but they can be addictive in themselves: they may persist after the original stress is removed. The best treatment then is to interrupt the behaviour and offer the dog something else interesting to do. But Betty was a dominant little dog and when Mrs B tried to interrupt her, she would growl and snap. Mrs B would then back off. I was a bit puzzled that Mrs B was so easily frightened as she seemed a determined, no-nonsense kind of woman. It probably had something to do with the fact that she was convinced that Betty had a brain tumour, though her vet and I had assured her that this was very unlikely.
>
> Because of this, the treatment reached an impasse. I suggested that Betty be admitted to the Clinic's hospital for a few days, so that we could study the behaviour. All the time Betty was with us, she behaved perfectly normally. She was a friendly little dog, with no scrabbling or growling. When Mrs B came to collect her and heard this, she was very cross. Although I assured her that it

was not unusual for an animal's behaviour problem to disappear temporarily with a change of surroundings, she obviously felt that Betty had made her look a fool. She left quickly, not stopping to discuss the problem any further. A few weeks later, she rang me to say that Betty was much better. She had discovered that the secret was to pick Betty up when she started growling and throw her onto a bed or sofa, saying, 'Stop your nonsense.' Though this was not a solution I would have recommended, because it was working for Mrs B, I endorsed it heartily. It seemed that once Mrs B had got over her inhibitions about tackling Betty when she was being aggressive, she was able to do it.

But the people who bear the heaviest responsibility are the breeders.

Recently I saw a breeder of Bernese mountain dogs – a large, powerful breed. He was a pleasant, sensible man who had taken up the hobby when he retired. One of his bitches was mounting such alarming attacks on another bitch, and on his wife, that they were contemplating euthanasia. I said that I was sure he realised that, whatever the outcome, he must not breed from her. He looked wistful and said that the vet had said the same thing and, if we said so, of course he wouldn't. But, he told me, it was a common problem in the breed, only no one would admit it. If someone had a dog like that, they just kept quiet about it.

The number of dangerous dogs in circulation would be substantially reduced if breeders refrained from breeding from dogs showing problematic aggression. Although the honourable few already do this, I am afraid that it will be some time before the majority are convinced of the necessity of it.

10 ● *Dirty Dogs*

Dangerous dogs hit the headlines from time to time. More staple fare for journalists are messy dogs – dogs who keep people awake at night with their barking, packs of dogs who raid dustbins, epidemics of dog fleas in the summer and, above all, dog faeces. Faeces is the central preoccupation of anti-dog groups such as the League for the Introduction of Canine Controls (LICC). Their logo features a defaecating dog. Their justification is Toxocara canis, the round-worm, which can be transmitted from dog to man via eggs excreted in dog faeces. The larvae of these worms can migrate through the body, occasionally causing blindness in humans. In publicity about dog faeces, such cases are always highlighted:

> Rachel Hall aged four has lost the sight of both eyes from toxocariasis. . . . She took part in the London (television) programme shown in July. This bright cheerful girl was filmed in a London park using a slide with confidence while chattering away to her mother. Mrs Hall says that Rachel never complains about her loss of sight . . . but she must leave her mother soon to go into a residential home for the blind in Liverpool. Mrs Hall's loving kiss as she cuddled her daughter made many of us cry with tears of sorrow and anger. (LICC newsletter, 1985)

Elsewhere in the same newsletter LICC accuses their adversaries, the 'Pro-dog lobby' of 'mawkish sentimentality'. It might be retorted that LICC themselves tread rather a fine line in this regard, but one can see what they mean. Talk of 'responsible owners' and images of Pat-dogs comforting the sick and elderly do seem rather rarefied when set against down-to-earth anti-dog publicity stunts such as sticking a plastic windmill into every pile of dog faeces in a park. J. R. Ackerley met complaints about dogs in parks with more robust arguments. In reply to an alderman's letter in a local newspaper he wrote:

> *What is the Alderman's notion of a suitable lavatory for a dog on Putney or Wimbledon Commons or any other common? And will he also tell us how we are to inform our dogs of its whereabouts? I wonder if he minds the birds, the squirrels, the Richmond Park deer defaecating? They do, you know. He and his complainants should be awfully careful about sitting on the grass in Kew Gardens anywhere near the lake where the large waterfowl wander about.*

And again in *My Dog Tulip*:

> *. . . The trouble with dogs is that they are not always inclined to relieve themselves when one desires them to do so . . . this truth, which is a general one, makes nonsense of all those official notices which request or command one to control one's dog in this respect. Indeed, I gaze with incredulity at the folly displayed by local councils in the posters and enamelled signs which they put up all over the place, regardless of expense. Putney is loaded with these signs, clamped to the stems of lamp-posts or screwed into walls, especially in the walls of alley-ways. They read: 'Wandsworth Borough Council. To dog owners. Please assist in maintaining PUBLIC HEALTH by restraining your dog from fouling footpaths. It is an offence to allow them to do so. The penalty being 40s.'*
>
> *Overlooking the peculiar grammar and punctuation of this piece of literature, what does it mean? Here is an alley way stretching ahead of me for two or three hundred yards. It is enclosed by high walls. There is no escape from it, except forwards or back. Dogs do not hold up their paws and say, 'May I?' They simply squat and begin. What do I do if Tulip suddenly squats in the middle of it? How does one restrain a dog who has begun? Anxious as I am to assist in maintaining PUBLIC HEALTH, I would be interested to know what method the Town Clerk would have me employ. The weakness of his position is visible both in the notice itself, which starts with a request and*

ends with a threat and in the fact that these alley ways are dotted with offences from end to end.

I remember seeing a young woman attempting to satisfy the requirements of the law. It was a moving spectacle. Her problem might seem simpler than the one I have set by placing Tulip in an alley; nevertheless she made a deplorable hash of it. The incident occurred at the north end of Sloane Street and I observed it comfortably from the top of a stationary bus. It was late in the morning, there were plenty of people about and the lady was walking below me with her poodle which was on a lead. As they were passing a cleaner's the dog was taken short. Quickly arranging his posterior against the wall of the shop, he began. With a sharp cry of dismay, his mistress hauled him across the broad pavement to the gutter. It cannot be pleasant to be dragged about by one's neck at such a moment. In any case the lady's interference could hardly have been more ill-timed and she was now convicted of earlier errors – she had been feeding her dog unwisely and too well. By the time he was in the gutter, he had finished and the side-walk was impassable. If only she had left the good, intelligent creature to his own modest devices, all would have been, if not well, then considerably better.

The above extract is from a chapter entitled 'Liquids and Solids' and shows why many readers found the book distasteful. The pro-dog lobby is perhaps better off without J. R. Ackerley to fight its corner, as he would undoubtedly antagonise the anti-dog lobby even more. But he would certainly have made the controversy more entertaining.

The reality of the matter is that dog faeces are not a great threat to human health. Another infection, toxoplasmosis, can also be transmitted to human beings via a parasite. In this case the live animal from which it is most commonly caught is the cat. About 50% of the population have antibodies to this infection, showing that they have caught it at some point in their lives. In most people it causes no symptoms, but in the unborn child it can cause blindness and brain damage. This disease does not cause much public concern because it is so rare: in Scotland about forty cases are reported every year. Compare this with toxocaria-sis: only 2–3% of the population have antibodies against this (the figure is 16% for dog breeders) and in Scotland only one or two cases are reported annually. Also compared with aggression in dogs or even barking toxocariasis is an easy problem to deal with. Adult dogs usually develop an immune response to the Toxocara canis larva, which arrests its development. These dogs do not excrete eggs. In pregnant bitches the immune response is depressed and the larvae migrate to the puppies via the placenta and later via the bitch's milk. It is these puppies who excrete eggs, but if they are wormed at intervals during the first year of life the parasite can be eradicated. There is also now a drug which can be given to the pregnant bitch to prevent her from passing the larvae on to the puppies. So the fuss about dog faeces is out of all proportion to the health risk. It is not a rational response, but an emotional one. It is presumably provoked by the unpleasantness and messiness of dog faeces.

The idea that the dog is a dirty animal is a very old one: the Old Testament Jews regarded the dog as unclean. It is also common to many cultures: Hindus and Moslems share the same attitude. Various reasons for this view of dogs have been proposed. The most plausible explanation seems to be that dogs are 'dirty' because they do 'dirty' things. In Eastern countries, pariah dogs in particular are forced to scavenge for food and therefore eat carrion, rotting food and human faeces. They are carriers of disease and are often diseased themselves. But it is important to bear in mind that the 'dirtiness' of dogs is a moral or ritual uncleanness not based primarily on rational considerations such as health risks. This distinction was illustrated by a story told to me by Monica Jackson, an anthropologist interested in dogs:

> Staying with some wealthy Hindu friends in India, she discovered that they had acquired a pet dog. They had been reluctant to take into their household a 'dirty' animal of this kind, but had been pressured into it by their children. Monica noticed that though the dog himself was

well cared for, he was allowed to mix freely with the pariah dogs in the neighbourhood. She also noticed that after supper the dirty dishes were left out in the courtyard for the servant to wash in the morning and the pet dog would regularly lick them. When, out of curiosity, she asked her friends if they did not consider this an unclean thing for the dog to do, they replied that, no, it was acceptable because their religion did not expressly forbid it.

When Monica returned to visit her friends a year later, the dog was gone. They explained that he had to be destroyed because he had caught rabies. Monica expressed her sympathy and said it must have been awful for their little son – whose dog it had been – especially as he would have had to undergo a series of painful rabies inoculations. They looked surprised and said they had not considered it necessary.

In any society, however well fed they are, dogs will eat things which people find repellent. They also do other things which are psychologically 'dirty'. They use their excretory functions also for the purpose of communication: they deposit their urine and faeces in prominent places; they sniff at one another's waste products and at one another's ano-genital regions. These smells give them information about a strange dog: its gender and reproductive status, for example. (Dogs who know one another well do not sniff one another's bottoms, they usually greet each other face to face.) As if all this were not shocking enough, dogs also upset people with their sexual habits. When a dog is courting or mating with a bitch, there is no mistaking what is going on and, including the tie, it can all take quite some time. Also, because of the social communication function of dogs' urine, this body fluid becomes part of the courting process in a way which human beings find particularly repulsive. J. R. Ackerley again, on a walk in the snow with Queenie (Tulip) in season:

> *Tulip . . . was in an ecstasy of joy; this was the first snow she had ever seen and warmly clad in her sable-grey coat, she flew*

about in it in childish glee. She was still bleeding a little: my most recent piece of lore on the subject was that dogs would not copulate with bitches till the flow of blood had ceased. Be that as it may, we were accompanied as usual by a small escort of ardent admirers. They did not trouble me much, however, partly because they all looked too small to be a serious menace, partly because she herself was so obedient. . . . I had already noticed that her urine, in her present condition, appeared to provide her wooers with a most gratifying cordial, for they avidly lapped it up whenever she condescended to void it, which she frequently did. So heady was its effect that their jaws would at once start to drip and chatter together, not merely visibly but audibly. Now, squatting here and there upon other dogs' droppings or whatever odour attracted her, like some famous chef adding to a prepared dish the final exquisite flavour, the crowning touch, she left behind her in the snow as she flew a series of sorbets, and her crazed attendants were so often and so long delayed in licking them up that they eventually fell far behind.

Passages like the above are a sophisticated form of lavatory humour, of the 'knickers and bums' jokes which convulse children at a certain age. Many jokes depend for their impact on the fact that they deal with sensitive and important issues. For all of us, early in our lives, urination and defaecation were sensitive and important issues. For a baby, defaecation especially produces a powerful physical sensation: you can tell that by looking at his face. He soon discovers that unlike feeding or being cuddled, which depend on the presence of his mother, this experience is controlled by him alone. This is particularly important around the age of two, when independence becomes a major issue. At this age children feel compelled to establish that they don't have to do what their mothers want. Around the same time, potty-training also is taking place. This very easily becomes another issue of conformity versus rebellion. But it is one which the child fights from a strong position: if he refuses to come indoors he can be picked up and carried in anyway, but no one can actually stop him urinating or defaecating when and where he wants to. If his mother feels relaxed about toilet training, she will wisely not make an issue out of it; the child will feel he is learning a useful and grown-up social accomplishment, rather than feeling he is submitting to authority. On the other hand, if the mother has a problem with mess and is determined to get her baby 'clean and dry' as quickly as possible, then the baby will discover he has enormous power both to please and to horrify her. Defaecation in the wrong place gives him a gratifying feeling of defiance in the short term. But it also makes him feel very guilty as he inevitably absorbs his mother's view of the matter. So long after toilet-training is completed, in fact for the rest of his life, he feels that defaecation and other forms of making a mess are exciting ways of asserting oneself, of undermining authority, but at the same time they are very wicked.

It is these people who as adults may become preoccupied with the issue of messy dogs. They have a permanent conflict between temptation to subvert authority by messing things up and their feelings of guilt at even imagining such a thing.

These people may use dogs in two contrasting ways. Some dogs haters feel so guilty about their own messy impulses that they project them into dogs in order to be rid of them. In contrast to these dirty dogs and their dirty owners, they can feel good and clean and pure. These are the people, like the members of LICC, who expend righteous energy persecuting and denouncing dogs. Others, dog owners, take secret pleasure in their dogs' messiness. Their dogs are an extension of themselves; to them, their dogs defaecating on the pavement is a satisfying act of defiance. There seems to be a touch of this attitude in Ackerley's defence of fouling dogs.

> It was even more clearly manifest in a middle-aged Morningside lady who used to pass our house each day with her West Highland white terrier. She would stand at the gate and watch while he trotted in and defaecated on our front grass. Once I realised what was going on, I used to watch out for her and if I saw her coming along the

road, I would go out into the garden and glare at her, until she had passed. This being Edinburgh, no word ever passed between us. I thought that she would be discouraged and look for another dog lavatory. In fact, judging by the evidence, it made things rather worse. She seemed to call more often and she must have taken active steps to evade my vigiliance: taking her walks early in the morning or doubling back as soon as I had gone inside.

But these two extreme groups need each other: those preoccupied with dog mess need those who use their dogs to be defiantly messy in order to fuel their anger legitimately; the defiantly messy need an angry person to defy.

Most people do not belong to either of these extreme camps. They feel revulsion if they step in dog faeces but the subject does not intrude on their waking thoughts at other times. If they are dog owners, they would prefer their dogs not to defaecate in anti-social places. As long as this reasonable majority steers the legislative process and makes the civic arrangements, then measures will prevail which keep dog fouling to a minimum and which dog owners find acceptable: keeping dogs out of children's play areas; encouraging owners to clear up after their dogs by providing, for example, poop scoops and waste bins. The minorities on either side, who are driven by primitive emotions, want unreasonable measures such as dogs allowed nowhere or dogs allowed everywhere. These measures antagonise large sections of the population and it is when these minorities are allowed to take charge that the trouble starts.

11 ● *Cruelty to Dogs*

People say that when you have children, you suddenly find unbearably upsetting pictures of starving babies in Africa and accounts in the newspapers of parents who neglect or abuse their children. This is true, but I also discovered that, as your children grow up, this area of special sensitivity changes with them. When they are teeenagers, it is no longer suffering babies which are particularly distressing, it is young people who have run away from home and are living rough. In contrast, I find that there is one type of story about cruelty or suffering which always upsets me, whatever my particular anxieties or preoccupations at the time: that is when animals are involved. I can hardly bear to watch television pictures of elephants being hunted for ivory, or dying parrots packed in a crate for export. The animals don't even have to belong to a species which I keep or have ever kept as pets. And it is not that I feel that concern for these animals should take precedence over concern about famine in Africa or about child abuse. It is just that the sight of these suffering animals provokes an automatic emotional response.

I know that I am not alone in having these feelings. A lot of people go much further.

> In the summer of 1991, the RSPCA rescued 500 beagles destined for laboratories, when the company which bred them went out of business. The dogs were healthy, but institutionalised. They didn't relate normally to people and were nervous out of their cages. In spite of the fact that their outlook as family pets did not seem promising,

the RSPCA appealed on television news for homes for
them: they had 700 inquiries of which 200 turned out to be
'genuinely interested'. Presumably the other 500
responded in the heat of the moment but, when it came
down to it, were not prepared to take on a real dog.

The British pride themselves on being a nation of 'animal-
lovers', but 150 years ago, things were very different. A
journalist wrote in 1825: 'Attached as we are to our native
land . . . we are bound to confess that the proverb is but
too true that "England is the hell of dumb animals".' And
in 1868, Queen Victoria wrote to her Home Secretary: 'The
English are inclined to be more cruel to animals than some
other civilised nations are.'

Public opinion changed gradually throughout the nineteenth century. The Society for the Prevention of Cruelty to
Animals (later the RSPCA) was founded in 1824 and a
series of anti-cruelty laws were passed in the following
decades. Nowadays the RSPCA is one of the charities
which everybody has heard about but it is still frustrated in
many of the cases which it brings to court. In February
1992, the *Edinburgh Evening News* reported the case of a
man who was prosecuted for neglecting his dog (see plates
13a and 13b).

> When the SSPCA [the Scottish equivalent of the RSPCA] were
> called in, the dog, whose condition was described as 'pitiful'
> weighed only two-thirds of what she should have done. She was
> also suffering from dermatitis and an infected cut on one leg. The
> owner was fined £250 . . . but Sheriff Roger Craig did not order
> that he should be banned from keeping the dog. Top animal
> welfare worker Ron Grant said, 'We felt it could mean we could
> be putting the dog back into the situation from which it had been
> rescued. It would defeat the whole thing if we had to hand her
> back. It has cost us around £700 to look after the dog since we
> rescued her, but we are getting no compensation at all.'

Also, very little work has been done to discover what
motivates people to be cruel to animals. But we know

something about the kind of people who carry out the abuse. Shona Watt, an animal behaviourist, studied SSPCA records over a three year period, which involved 215 cases of cruelty to pets. She divided the offences into three categories: abuse (i.e. violence), neglect (failing to provide the animal with such things as food, water or veterinary treatment) and abandonment (leaving the animal somewhere or going away without making arrangements for its care). Three-quarters of the cases involved dogs: of these, 66% were neglected, 13% were abused and 10% were abandoned. Almost all the abusers were men but dogs were neglected or abandoned by men and women in equal proportions. The majority of people who abused or abandoned their animals were under 35 years old, whereas neglect was spread evenly across all age groups.

Crimes of violence against animals, therefore, like crimes of violence against people, tend to be carried out by young men. This kind of cruelty attracts the most attention, both popular and scientific. There is some evidence from American studies to suggest that the two kinds of violence are associated. Violent prisoners and psychiatric patients both report a higher incidence of childhood abuse of animals, compared with non-violent prisoners or patients. There is also evidence that some kinds of abuse of animals may be a sinister sign of deep disturbance in the personality. Many serial killers started off their careers by torturing and killing animals. For example, Albert DeSalvo, the Boston strangler, in his youth trapped dogs and cats in orange crates and shot arrows through the boxes. These studies of violent men who abused animals also found that most of the men were subjected, as children, to extreme parental brutality.

Although not so much attention is paid to those who neglect animals, what evidence there is suggests that they follow a pattern similar to the violent abusers. Stuart Hutton, an English social worker, looked at sixteen families reported to the RSPCA in his area. He found that fourteen were also known to the social services. Where ill-treatment of children was involved, the type of ill-treatment matched that of the animals: where the animals were neglected, the children tended to be neglected also.

> This is illustrated by a case reported in the press of a mother who went away for the weekend leaving in the house her two-year-old daughter and a Dobermann. My reaction when I read the bit about the Dobermann was that at least the child had some company. But this happened during the 1991 dangerous dog scare and the general reaction of the media seemed to be that leaving the dog in the house made the mother's action even more morally reprehensible: not because of the suffering caused to the dog, but because of the supposed danger to the child.

Conversely, an American study found that in families where children were abused or neglected, the same thing tended to happen to the pets. Unlike the prisoners or the psychiatric patients – who, being in an institution, perhaps welcomed the researcher's interest and also felt they had nothing to lose by admitting childhood acts of cruelty – many of these families often concealed their ill-treatment of pets and the researcher had to infer it, for example:

> *Mrs G said she gave the two dogs water three to four times daily. However, the animals never had food or water available to them (during the interviewer's visits) even on the hottest summer days.*

Because of this association it has been suggested that pet ill-treatment could act as a warning sign to social workers.

> *In July 1989* The Times *reported the case of the toddler Doreen Mason, who died of a brain haemorrhage as a result of either being thrown against a wall or dropped on the floor. Before her death, the family dog had been rescued by the RSPCA. 'A muzzle had been fastened so tightly that it dug into four or five*

levels of skin. Doreen's mother and step-father admitted to throwing the dog against the wardrobe.'

The RSPCA Chief Inspector, Jan Eachus, was called to the scene. He sensed that there was something wrong with Doreen too: it was a hot day but Doreen was bundled up in clothes. 'She was cranky, crying. The mother was extremely irritable and at one time ran out of the flat,' the inspector remembers. Eachus notified the social services and they informed him they were aware of the family and would follow up the case. 'Weeks later I got a call from Kennington CID at 11 o'clock at night asking if I had got anything on the family,' Eachus says. Doreen had died in hospital.

This is horrific stuff but it is also strangely reassuring. It gives us a feeling that those who ill-treat pets are Bad People. They are monsters, violent men, neglecting women, not at all like us and easily recognisable – there is no danger that we could turn into one or even be friends with one. Harriet Ritvo points out that the Victorians employed a similar mental manoeuvre when they identified cruelty to animals with the under-class of society.

The annual report of the RSPCA for 1838 records that London dog pits were 'the rendezvous of the lowest class', that they attracted a crowd of 'many gentlemen's servants and coachmen as also thieves and blackguards of the lowest kind'. They tried to explain away facts which did not fit in with this view. Thus, at a dog fight, policemen found 'several persons dressed as gentlemen' and bull-baiting crowds sometimes included 'persons who call themselves respectable'.

Although it is reassuring, this view of animal cruelty is also unsatisfying. To condemn the behaviour and see it as being carried out by people quite unlike ourselves gives us no insight into its motivation. Why are people cruel to animals? To answer this, I think one must begin by accepting that the above view is a gross over-simplification. As the SSPCA inspectors whom I talked to emphasised, all kinds of people ill-treat animals, not just obviously disturbed people or obviously chaotic families. In my work, I do not often come across owners who abuse or neglect their dogs in any gross way, but when I do come across them, the dogs I feel most sorry for are not those who live in disorganised or impulsive families who may kick their dogs one minute, but will cuddle them the next. The systematic abuse I come across tends to be carried out by cold, over-controlled owners – not happy people, certainly, but not people who would obviously attract attention from the social services.

> One example was a woman in her thirties who consulted me about her Labrador. Her husband was a business man and she was neatly and expensively dressed in leather and cashmere. Her account of her domestic arrangements included a large house, many cars, a horse etc. The trouble with the dog was that he tended to rush out when visitors arrived, barking aggressively. For this reason, he was confined to an out-house – all the time. When I suggested that he might not be very happy there, she looked surprised and said that when it was cold she lit the paraffin heater.

Anthropologists have also been surprised by how viciously an otherwise peaceful and easy-going people can behave towards animals. For example, Jean Briggs spent two years with the Utku Eskimos who live in north-west Canada. She found them an extremely gentle and considerate people, who were appalled by the selfishness and displays of bad temper shown by the 'kapluna' (foreigners) with whom they came in contact. But the Utku's treatment of their dogs contrasted sharply with the rest of their behaviour:

> *All the Utku beat their dogs; they saw it as a necessary disciplinary measure: 'We all do it; we know it makes the dogs behave; everybody knows it,' they emphasised in justification. They beat them with boots, rocks, frozen fish, hammers, tent-*

poles or anything else which came to hand, and as the dog was usually chained or harnessed, escape was impossible. They got a good deal more than pedagogical satisfaction out of the process, too; I saw gleaming eyes and smiles of delight as dogs cowered and whined with bruises and bloody heads. I also saw a woman's face absolutely set and expressionless as she pounded and pounded a thieving dog from a distance of two or three feet with a boulder, which she picked up and threw again every time it bounced off the animal's ribs. . . . The children enjoyed killing the newborn unwanted puppies, dashing them with squeals of excited laughter against the boulders or throwing them off a high knoll edge into the rapids below.

Concentrating on shocking and criminal acts of cruelty allows us conveniently to ignore the more minor but much more widespread acts of cruelty which, as I shall argue, we and other dog lovers constantly carry out. If it is meaningful to quantify such things, it could be argued that the total amount of suffering caused to dogs by these minor cruelties is much greater than that caused by the rare criminal cases.

There is one study of criminal cruelty which does help us to understand the motives behind it. In the study which showed a connection between general violence and animal abuse in criminals, Stephen Kellert and Alan Felthous interviewed the animal abusers in some depth. They discovered several kinds of motive for the abuse. A similar range of motives underlies the milder, more everyday forms of cruelty.

Some acts of violence have the aim of punishing the victim. Sometimes the rationalisation is offered that it will make the dog behave better in the future. The Utku Eskimos are an example of this; also the subject in Kellert and Felthous's study who 'kicked his dog in the testicles because it bothered him at the dinner table'; and the one who 'repeatedly rubbed his dog's anus in turpentine to dissuade it from entering the chicken coop'. Sometimes – since the dog does not survive – there can be no pretence of improving the dog's behaviour: the act is pure retaliation.

The Dobermann in Chapter 9 who was fed a piece of poisoned meat by a man whom he threatened is an example of this. Also the subjects who 'shot and killed a dog which tried to mate with his dog' and 'drowned a neighbour's dog for barking too much'.

This kind of pointless retaliation on a smaller scale is widespread among dog owners. When a dog does something the owner objects to, more often than not the first thing that the owner tries is punishment. It should be the method of last resort, because, as experimental studies have shown, punishment is an unreliable way of changing behaviour. There are various reasons for this (see *Problem Dog*) but one is that it increases anxiety, thus making learning more difficult. Also, the dog may easily become confused as to what aspect of his behaviour he is being punished for: smacking a puppy when he urinates on the carpet in front of you may teach him not to urinate when you are around, rather than teaching him not to urinate on the carpet. A much more reliable way of eradicating problem behaviour is to distract or prevent the dog from misbehaving and, in addition, provide him with some acceptable alternative: the puppy should be taken outside before he makes his puddle on the carpet and encouraged to form the habit of urinating on a particular piece of ground.

Punishment is so popular, not because it is effective, but because it is psychologically satisfying for the owners. If we return home to find that the dog has disembowelled a cushion in our absence, it requires great self-control to clear up the mess without comment, while the dog looks on with interest. It feels much more appropriate to shout at him or hit him, so that at least he cowers in the corner while we do the clearing up. One reason why punishment is so satisfying is that it shifts the blame completely off us and puts it fairly and squarely on the dog. If the dog is bad or naughty, then we are spared from having to attribute the problem behaviour to our own mistakes. Of course, a lot of problems are no one's fault, but we often have a need to find someone to blame. This need is especially strong if the dog does something which we ourselves feel guilty about doing. It is even stronger if there is a third party around who has been harmed by the behaviour. We then often feel an overwhelming need to distance ourselves from the dog.

> Mr and Mrs M were considering having Maggie, their West Highland white terrier, destroyed, because she sometimes ran out to visitors on the doorstep and bit them on the ankle. Mr M had an unsettling manner: his only contribution to the interview was to flick the dog's lead to and fro in his hand in a slightly menacing way and to shoot glances of what felt like extreme dislike at his wife and myself in turn. Mrs M was nervous and self-effacing: she automatically agreed to everything I said in a way which made me wonder what she was really thinking. Her method of dealing with Maggie's behaviour up until then had been either to shut her away in the kitchen (where she had no chance of learning good manners) or to 'wallop her and wallop her' after her displays of aggression. When she described these wallopings a faint gleam came into her eyes.
>
> I felt that a lot of blaming probably went on in the M household and that an outbreak on the part of Maggie was one of the few occasions when Mrs M could decisively shift that blame off her own shoulders. But what made Maggie's behaviour intolerable to Mrs M was that outsiders tended to criticise Mrs M for it. Neighbours would come into the village shop and complain that Maggie, who was tied up outside, had growled at them when they patted her. Mrs M also used the walloping to dissociate herself from the growling and show that she condemned it.

Often when a dog becomes a scapegoat in this way, another dog in the household is seen as the 'good' dog and is never punished. There is usually some basis in reality for this, in that the 'bad' dog does show more problematic behaviour, but the matter is often not as clear-cut as the owner likes to believe. An owner may describe to me how one of his two dogs chews things up or urinates on the floor when left alone. When I ask him how he knows that it is always the same dog, it often seems to me he has not enough evidence to be sure.

The need to find a scapegoat is often particularly pressing in people who have been abused as children. These children tend to feel very guilty; they feel that they must be very bad to deserve to be treated that way. They therefore have a correspondingly urgent wish to be rid of this guilt. This is why such a person is more likely to abuse animals. When he punishes a dog, he can feel, at least temporarily, that it is the dog, rather than he, who is bad.

Another category of violent abuse is expressing aggression through an animal. We have already seen some examples of this in Chapter 9 in people who find satisfaction in owning 'dangerous' dogs. In some instances, the dog's aggression puts itself as well as others at risk. The best-known example – and rightly so – of cruelty of this kind is dog-fighting. In 1986 the American Humane Society published a report on this:

> *While the American pit bull terrier – the most commonly fought breed – averages only about 40–50 pounds, its jaws are extraordinarily muscular and are capable of breaking an opponent's leg in a matter of seconds. Due to generations of selective breeding for a combative disposition, along with a gruelling training regimen that cultivates the animal's blood instincts, it is virtually impossible to keep fighting dogs from attacking each other once they have eyed an opponent.*
>
> *To begin a contest, both dogs are carried into a makeshift pit – a 20 foot square plywood ring with two and a half foot walls – and placed in their respective corners. On the referee's command of 'face your dogs' the animals are turned towards each other and with the words 'let go!' are released to square off in what is often a fight to the death.*
>
> *Once an animal has a firm hold on another, jaws lock in place. To start with, the dog with the hold savagely tears and shakes his competitor, blood and urine spatter everywhere, staining pit walls, carpet, even the referee's clothing. Despite serious injuries incurred early on in the match – puncture wounds, large gashes,*

broken bones and internal injuries – these animals will continue to grapple with each other, often until they collapse or are dragged out of the pit.

Ashamed of a losing dog, an owner may destroy his animal with a bullet to the brain or a knife to the throat . . . the fact is that losers aren't the only ones that die. According to insiders, more than 50% of all dogs involved in a match die within days or weeks of a fight from the injuries they have sustained. That's not surprising, however, considering that dog fighters can't run to the vet with the battered animal for fear of being turned over to the authorities. Instead, using tape or catgut to close up gaping wounds, owners do the job themselves. According to one dog fighter interviewd by the Los Angeles Times, *'We carry all the equipment and stitch them up right there. If they're bleeding a lot we put pepper or coffee grounds on the wounds to make the bleeding stop.'*

Unfortunately, the cruelties of dog fighting aren't confined to the pit nor are they limited to the animals that compete. Rather, the road to the dog fight begins at puppy stage. It is then that kittens are dangled before – then ravaged by – young pit bulls in an effort to whet their appetites for blood. When a dog reaches about two years of age, it is ready to begin its fighting career. For more than a month before a fight, dogs are maintained on rigid diets and pushed to their endurance limits (see plate 14). Extremely popular among trainers is the 'cat-mill', a wheel-like device which resembles a miniature horse-walker. A dog, chained to one spoke, frantically chases a cat fastened to a spoke just out of its reach. After hours of pursuing the bait, the dog receives it as a reward.

This makes ghastly reading and there is no doubt that every effort should be made to stamp out this practice. But horror at these kinds of goings-on should not prevent us from being critical or self-critical about less extreme activities: activities which, although perfectly legal, have similar motivation and the same flavour. Anne Roslyn-Williams, who writes regularly in *Dog World*, writes in her book, *The Border Terrier*:

Once a puppy has fully changed its teeth, it may start learning to worry an old sock or rag attached firmly to a strong piece of

string. . . . The next step is to put the rag somewhere the puppy
will have to go either into or under, such as a dog kennel or hen
house. . . . By holding the string and jerking at the right time,
the youngster can be made to believe that it is alive and needs
killing. When the pup is 'killing', I make realistic squeaking
noises in the universal language of terrier men and terriers, the
prolonged hissing, which being translated means 'Get in and get
'im'. . . . From this the youngster progresses to rats. Should one
have rats around fodder bins, by leaving the lid of one of these
bins open when the level of food is low in the bin, one can create
the ideal opportunity for the youngster to meet his first rat, there
often being a couple of young rats at the bottom of the bin in the
morning . . . half-grown rats are the best to start a youngster as
the mommas and poppas can take some handling and can give a
nasty bite if not dispatched immediately. . . . The young terrier
may not like being dropped into a dark bin but the lid must be
quickly replaced, otherwise the rats will use the terrier as a
ladder to freedom. . . .

   It is more difficult to find work for terriers than gun-dogs as
one cannot take the terrier work in a district as one can a shoot.
The local hunt will make its own arrangements for terrier work,
but if one appears frequently . . . the opportunity may present
itself. . . . A youngster is best sent in to follow an experienced
terrier for the first time. . . . The older terrier can show him by
demonstrating what to do when confronted by Reynard. . . . It is
quite amazing the amount of punishment a Border will take and
equally amazing the speed at which even the most ghastly bites
will heal. . . . I am a great believer in disinfecting all bites – they
are sore anyway – so I am fairly free with the disinfectant. This
applies to all bites but especially to rat bites.

I am not implying that this kind of thing is on a par with
dog-fighting or even that it is bad thing, rather, I want to
make the point that the encouragement and enjoyment of a
dog's natural aggressive instincts – even if it means he gets
hurt in the process – is not confined to the high-profile
cruel owners.

Another common form of animal abuse is displaced
aggression. In one form of this, the abuser attacks the dog's
owner through his dog. A story which appeared in *Dog
World* in July 1991 is an example of this:

A jilted lover angrily swung his girlfriend's four-month-old puppy after storming round to her mother's address, Old Street Magistrate's Court heard. He arrived at his ex-girlfriend's address, where she was staying with her mother, on May 4th last year, when there was a confrontation outside. 'He started swinging the dog in circles, he threatened to kill it, he put it under his arm and pushed its head hard against his chest,' said the mother of Finsbury Park.

Sometimes this can have consequences which the attacker did not foresee.

Mrs P, a woman in her thirties, and recently separated from her husband, consulted me about Prince, her young German shepherd. The problem that she was having with him was that he would growl at visitors to her flat or people she stopped to speak to in the street. This behaviour had started during the rows which led up to the break-up of the marriage. When he got angry with Mrs P, Mr P would shout at and hit Prince. Prince did not meekly submit to this, however, but would give as good as he got. Then gradually this protectiveness generalised to people who were not being hostile at all.

In a slightly different version of this kind of cruelty, the abuser, having himself been on the receiving end of aggression which he cannot defend himself against, passes the aggression on to an animal which cannot defend itself. The victim tries to make himself feel better by taking on the role of the aggressor.

An American psychotherapist, Bennett Roth, reports an example of this in the treatment of one of his patients. A young woman recalled that in her childhood her mother had severe 'temper tantrums' and was frequently depressed. Often if her daughter approached her she would strike out and chase her into her room. 'She confessed in one tearful session that when she was in the house alone as an adolescent child, she would lure the family dogs into her room, encourage the dogs to approach her, begin to fondle and pet them, then

suddenly hurl them against the wall. Each dog never
forgave her and if she approached them, they would circle
round her. She was afraid to have a dog or child of her
own for fear she would repeat the pattern of abuse again.'

So it is not surprising that not only do abused children tend
to abuse animals, but also (as a study by an American social
worker Michael Robin has shown) more of their own pets
have been killed or abused by members of their own
families. One teenage boy in institutional care because of
delinquency reported, 'My brother wouldn't take care of
[my dog] because I got sent here, so he shot him.'

This degree of displaced aggression is shocking to us,
but in its milder forms it is very common. My impression is
that very few of us could swear that we have never shouted
at a dog after an unsatisfactory row with our spouses or
have never felt dislike towards a dog, not because of what
the dog itself did, but because it belonged to a person we
disliked.

Another category of cruelty described by Kellert and
Felthous is 'non-specific sadism' – cruelty for its own sake.
This is the kind carried out as 'practice' by future serial
killers. It seems certain, however, that this sadism is not
accompanied by the same state of mind in all the per-
petrators: it can be the result of a whole variety of bizarre
mental processes. In contrast to the other forms of cruelty,
these can be hard to understand or empathise with. For
example, one of Kellert and Felthous's subjects was fascin-
ated with the boundary between life and death:

> He compared his curiosity about killing chickens with Leonardo
> da Vinci's interest in watching humans being guillotined.
> Chicken brains, he reasoned, like humans', must be aware
> momentarily after the head is severed.

Other evidence about these kinds of mental states comes
indirectly from interviews with people who have acted in
the same kind of sadistic way towards other people, for

example, the Nazis working in concentration camps. Some of these have a feeling of deadness inside themselves; causing extreme pain or suffering in others is the only way they know of making themselves feel alive again. (Similar motivation is seen in some patients who hurt themselves, commonly by burning themselves with cigarettes or slashing their arms with a razor; they often say that they do this in order to feel alive.)

Extreme sadism can also gratify a need to be in control. Torturing or killing a person or animal demonstrates to the perpetrator how completely the victim is at his mercy. People who feel this need have usually been subjected as children to abuse so horrendous that they themselves carry with them a feeling of being completely at the mercy of malign forces. The fear which this produces can only be removed by reversing the roles.

One factor contributing to abuse, not mentioned by Kellert and Felthous – perhaps because it is a reason rather than a motive – is the inability of the abuser to control or contain his feelings. Rather than just feeling angry and doing nothing or expressing his aggression in words, he lashes out physically. This can be a permanent personality trait – it is often learnt from parents who behave in the same way. It can also happen to any of us when we are under stress. In a case reported in *Dog World*, July 1991, a breeder tried to excuse her conduct by saying she was under pressure of this kind (the story is confusing at times, because both accuser and accused recruit as many people as possible to support their point of view):

> Kitty Wharton, former secretary of Slough CS and a member of the British Dalmatian Club committee, has been banned for five years by a Kennel Club disciplinary hearing. She was also fined £100 and ordered to pay £100 costs. She had admitted the claim in a complaint against her that she hit Rona, an eight-month-old Dalmatian pup, and lifted it by the tail until it screamed in pain at the British Utility Breeds CH Show last December.
> Mrs Monica Davidson was so upset by what she saw that she

lodged a complaint, supported by a petition of people at the show, containing 23 names. But when the complaint came before the disciplinary panel, Mrs Davidson was unable to prosecute it herself because she had lost her voice. Instead, Miss Susan Gatherall . . . acted as her spokesperson. Miss Gatherall told the panel, 'I confirm that I was a witness to a display of bad temper.' Questioned by Mrs Wharton as to how she thought what she had done was in temper, Miss Gatherall replied, 'I think it is perfectly obvious that it was done in temper. The puppy was jumping around and not misbehaving in any way and I was within six feet of this incident.'

Miss Davidson, through Miss Gatherall, told the panel that Mrs Wharton suddenly struck the puppy very hard blows to the head and picked it up by the tail, lifting it clear of the ground, whereupon the puppy cried out in pain. Mrs Davidson claimed that Mrs Wharton showed no signs of shame and 'used a few choice swear words'. There were overseas visitors, newcomers to shows and others who witnessed the event, said Mrs Davidson. She added, 'In thirty years I have never seen Mrs Wharton handle her dogs in a gentle manner.'

Mrs Wharton, who told the hearing she was 71 . . . [said] she had been out of the country from September 30th to November 27th in Australia, judging. During this time, the puppy, Rona, had been with her partner, but she was pregnant with her second child and therefore unable to spend the time with her. (It is difficult at times to tell who did what and to whom.) She returned 'terribly exhausted' after a very long flight of thirty-six hours because of the Gulf War. She was sleeping by day and unable to sleep at night. Rona, she said, was 'very excited', but she and Rona spent a quiet day on the Friday and though she went to bed, could not sleep. On December 1st she was taken to the show by friends and 'I talked all the way about the trip.' She took Rona in the ring in Minor Puppy class and 'she was jumping about like a fish on a line. I did smack the dog twice and I did hold her by the tail. I was terribly exhausted and I did not know what I was doing.'

Even an animal lover such as Winston Churchill was prone to this kind of behaviour when under pressure:

One of his secretaries tells how, during World War II, he used to conduct matters of state from his bed with his pets around him. One morning, when he was on the telephone, a favourite cat pounced on his wiggling toes. In an explosion of irritation, he swore and kicked the cat off the bed, much mystifying the caller at the other end of the line. He was then overcome with remorse and exclaimed, 'Oh poor thing,' thus mystifying the caller even further.

As I have already mentioned, suffering caused to dogs by neglect has received comparatively little attention, in spite of the fact that five times as many dogs are neglected as are abused. But it seems likely that, in many cases, similar mental mechanisms are involved in neglect and in abuse. Also, minor, non-criminal forms of neglect are just as prevalent as abuse among dog owners.

We have seen how, by punishing their dogs, owners play 'pass the parcel' with their own feelings of guilt and badness. Another unpleasant parcel of feelings – those involving helplessness and dependency – are passed on to dogs by neglecting or abandoning them. We saw in Chapter 4 how owners can induce separation anxiety in their dogs because they inappropriately see them as parents, as individuals on whom they depend, rather than the other way round. Another reason for leaving a dog alone for an intolerable length of time is to rid oneself of the unbearable feeling of needing and missing someone else. Owners who have this kind of motivation often pride themselves on their own self-reliance and are impatient of weakness and clinginess in others. This is not to say that dogs or puppies should never be left on their own; but separations should be introduced sensitively and gradually. This idea is intensely irritating to those who are intolerant of their own feelings of dependency. To them, the puppy's distress at being left alone in the kitchen at night is a necessary part of the process, because, without it, the 'pass-the-parcel' mental manoeuvre could not take place.

As with violent abuse, people may neglect or abandon dogs in order to hurt those who love them. In the following case, the line between neglect, abandonment and violence is a fine one. A teacher in her forties writes of her difficult relationship with her mother:

> *There is no doubt that my mother loved my brother and I, but was such a possessive woman and one who had to be the centre of attention and to have her own way at any cost, that my brother and I were very controlled all our lives. We both stayed at home because of my father, who was a wonderful man but confined to a wheelchair. When he died, my brother left home and I, who was not so quick off the mark, so to speak, was left with my mother. She made the house over to my name, in order to keep me at home and things proceeded stormily for 20 years. Finally I decided to sell the house and the trouble really started. She spurned all offers of help and ripped the fittings from the ceiling, threw plants on the floor and started to destroy the garden shed – burning great chunks of it in the middle of the lawn. She made several attempts to take my dog and throw him into the road, where he would undoubtedly have been injured, as he has no road sense. I was reduced to putting him in a kennel on the way to work each day and picking him up on the way home in order to keep him safe.*

(The capacity of dreams to encapsulate a problem is illustrated beautifully in this owner's dream: 'picking a puppy from the gutter and taking it into house – mother refusing to let me keep it.')

As with 'non-specific sadism', there are undoubtedly some cases of neglect which are prompted by bizarre states of mind, some of these producing the need to have absolute control over someone else.

> In one case of neglect described to me by the SSPCA Chief Inspector in Edinburgh a man bought an Alsatian and kept him in a cupboard, where he eventually died of thirst and starvation. He was successfully prosecuted over this incident, but immediately afterwards acquired another dog and repeated the procedure. It seemed that the man lived with his sister and was very much under her thumb. She would not tolerate dogs, so this dog-owning was an act of defiance: he would boast to his mates about his

dogs. Keeping them starving in a cupboard was presumably a strategy for concealing them from his sister. But there is something bizarre about it too: it sounds as if it may also have been a method of exercising a life-and-death power over them.

As with violence, neglect can be the result of things simply getting on top of an owner:

> *Newfoundland breeder Rosemary Miller and her husband were banned from owning dogs for three years and fined £1,000 by Sussex magistrates. They admitted a series of charges of causing unnecessary suffering to a total of forty dogs. After his visit, the RSPCA inspector had reported 'an overpowering stench' caused by the build-up of excrement in the kennels. Newfoundland dogs were seen with dirty and soiled coats and faeces had been allowed to accumulate in the kennels up to an average of half an inch deep. Water left for the animals appeared stagnant and dirty. There was 'substantial evidence of mould on the faeces which had been left for a considerable time'. Fleas and lice were evident amid the filth and squalor.*
>
> *Defending, Mr Howard Ogden described the case as a tragedy and 'a great embarrassment and a loss of status for Mrs Miller'. He said that she had made a valuable contribution to the Newfoundland breed, had taken in a number of dogs for rescue and had given her services to animal charities. Two litters of puppies were born in the week preceding the visit to the kennels by the RSPCA inspector. The result had been 17 puppies and attending to their needs had become a 24-hour job for Mrs Miller. 'She simply could not cope with the responsibilities involved single-handedly and that was where standards had declined,' he said. Mr Ogden said the couple had obtained planning permission for quarantine kennels at their home but the company to whom they had paid a £30,000 construction fee had gone bankrupt.'* (Dog World, June 1991)

Except for these cases where cruelty is the unintentional result of general chaos in the owner's life, the one common element in all this catalogue of abuse and neglect is that part of the point, for the perpetrator, is that the animal should suffer. Punching a teddy bear or keeping a car short of petrol would not feel the same. But there are other forms of cruelty which result from deliberately disregarding the feelings or needs of the dog, treating it as if it were an object. It is only compartively recently that we have ceased to regard all animals, all the time, as objects. In the seventeenth century, Descartes was typical of his time in proposing that animals were only machines. A contemporary eye-witness reported that his followers

> *administered beatings to dogs with perfect indifference and made fun of those who pitied the creatures as if they felt pain. They said the animals were clocks, that the cries they emitted when struck were only the noise of a little spring that had been touched, but that the whole body was without feeling.*

Although, as we have seen, concern about cruelty towards animals increased during the nineteenth century, the Victorians were still convinced of their own superiority over and difference from other animals. They found Darwin's theories shocking. Today, by and large, we still treat farm animals as if they were objects.

Breeders, and the dog world generally, condemn people whom they call 'puppy-farmers' for profiting at the expense of their dogs' suffering: breeding bitches at every season, keeping puppies in cramped conditions and so on. But many 'competition' owners of multiple dogs are guilty of the same kind of exploitation, even if the aim is not money but self-aggrandisement. If you are breeding for show, then, unless you live in a palace, you have a numbers problem. The more litters you breed, the higher your chances of breeding a champion. Because it is often not possible to predict how a young puppy will turn out, puppies frequently have to be 'run on' for up to a year before they go to new owners. Many breeders deal with the problem by keeping their dogs as zoo animals rather than as pets. When I took Kirsty to her ill-fated mating with Phantastic, I was taken aback to see, in the tiny kitchen of the bungalow, seven or eight Cavaliers in wire cages. Bigger dogs are often kept outside, in runs. This must severely reduce their quality of life. In addition, many breeders alleviate the problem by finding new homes for dogs or bitches who are past their showing or breeding prime. This cannot be very satisfactory for the dogs concerned who, even if they have not formed a close tie with their breeder/owner, are accustomed to living in a family of dogs rather than a family of people. If they have lived in kennels or cages, they may also present their new owners with problems of house training.

Breeders may also exploit their dogs by forcing on them a physical appearance which is not in their best interests. Ear-cropping is no longer carried out in this country, because vets won't do it. But tail-docking is still a hot issue. Since July 1993, only vets can legally dock dogs' tails. Breeders suspect – probably rightly – that most vets will then refuse to do it for other than medical reasons. Breeders are furious about this; you can buy pro-docking teeshirts and dog papers return to the issue again and again. Bizarre arguments are sometimes invoked, as in the correspondence column in *Dog World*, 6 September 1991:

> *As a former nurse, I have attended many operations on tiny babies to remove little fingers and toes for purely cosmetic purposes. It does streamline the feet and make gloves easier to wear if one has only ten fingers and ten toes. As to noses, thousands are bobbed every year because they are considered unsightly. Nor is one required to be a surgeon to circumcise male babies at a few days old. I recollect that the most famous male to approve of circumcision could walk on water.*

To an outsider, it may not be immediately obvious why breeders are so keen to mutilate their puppies. The answer is that they are opposed to any interference with their right to control and modify their dogs' appearances at will. But they also modify their dogs' appearance in a way which is harder for vets or anyone else to interfere with: by selective breeding. The physical deformities and disabilities which this process produces are well-known: for example, long backs giving rise to spinal problems, short noses producing breathing difficulties and large heads making Caesarean section almost routine in some breeds.

From the dog's point of view, a medium-sized mongrel is the healthiest thing to be. So why, over the centuries, have breeders distorted this serviceable, wolf-like shape in so many bizarre ways? The conformations of some of the breeds did originally serve some purpose. The short legs of dachshunds, for instance, enabled them to hunt badgers in their sets. The undershot jaw and pushed-in nose of the bulldog enabled it to get a good grip with its jaws. But few dogs today make use of these distinctive physical features, which anyway, in many cases, have been exaggerated past the point of usefulness. Pedigree dogs are rather like high-fashion training shoes which are useless for running in, or knee-high boots which let the water in. Quite frequently, too, an owner's choice of breed is influenced by the same sort of considerations which come into the choice of fashion footwear: a certain breed is chosen because its image fits in with the owner's ideal image of himself. The most obvious examples which spring to mind are the actress photographed at home, posing with her Afghan on a deep pile carpet, or would-be tough men with Rottweilers or bull terriers. But I suspect, that, apart from the Noah's Ark owners – who don't give a damn what the rest of the world thinks – most of us are conscious to some extent of the message our dog conveys to the world around us. Retrievers and Labradors, for example, convey the message that their owners are clean-living, 'upper-class' people who take healthy exercise; Alsatians that their owners are street-wise and masters of their own destiny. Little hairy terriers are popular with the Scots, because the Scots like to see themselves as small, tough and independent. Some breeds project conflicting images: owners of Pekingese perhaps see themselves as Chinese emperors;

onlookers are more often put in mind of Tricki-woo and Mrs Pumphrey in *All Creatures Great and Small*. The images of some breeds are harder to decipher. Old English sheep dogs, for example; it is difficult to see why people would want a dog which looks as if it can't see where it's going. It is said that the Dulux advertisements have made the breed popular. Do their owners really want to be seen as people who do a lot of house painting with their dog getting in the way?

However, the major responsibility for the deformities of various breeds must fall on the breeders. They could produce dogs with less exaggerated physical features – shorter backs, longer legs and longer noses – and still satisfy consumer demand for differently packaged varieties. But, even more than the ordinary dog owner, breeders need these differences. Their identities are even more predicated on their dogs. If breeds became indistinguishable from one another, the whole structure of breed societies and competition between breeds would collapse. This fact acts as a sort of centrifugal force which, unopposed, leads to the differences between breeds becoming more and more exaggerated (see plate 15).

Fortunately, there are signs that, in both breeders and owners, forces opposed to this centrifugal force are stirring. The shift in public opinion in favour of the green and the natural and against the artificial and contrived seems to be starting to curb the worst excesses of the breeders. For example, when the shar-pei was introduced into Britain a few years ago, public disgust was expressed (for example, in 'Blue Peter') at the problems produced by its wrinkled skin, which is liable to irritation and infection. And some breed societies seem to be responding to this kind of pressure and, in their breed standards, taking the physical well-being of the dog a little more into account.

It may seem perverse to carp about these minor forms of cruelty which are carried out by people, most of whom, after all, love dogs in their own ways, when there are at large people like puppy-farmers and sadistic monsters who neglect and torture dogs in much more extreme ways. Of course, efforts must be made to stop the activities of these really cruel people. But only the law can stop people like puppy-farmers who do not care about public opinion. And even the law seems to have little effect on sadists or serial killers: they are driven by their own bizarre psychopathology and feel alienated from society anyway. People like breeders, on the other hand, who feel themselves to be integrated into society and whose activities are approved by society, can be influenced by public opinion. It is up to ordinary dog owners to tell them what they think of them.

Part IV
The End of Life and Beyond

Tina passed away within five weeks of becoming ill. She had caught a kidney virus and then it went to her limbs and then it went to her heart. The vet tried to save her but when it got to the heart they said they could do nothing and three days before she went she was on seventeen tablets and on the day she died she could not eat and at 10.15 at night she just died on the mat by my fire. You may think this was daft but just before Tina went I said to her if she wanted to go now as there were no hope I would see her in heaven and just as I said it she looked at me and went as though I had given her peace. (Maureen, aged thirty-seven)

Because a dog's normal life-span is so much shorter than ours, most dog-lovers have the kind of experience described above several times in their dog-owning life-time. To a certain extent, this sadness is an inevitable consequence of loving the dog in the first place – part of life's rich pattern, if you like. But some owners suffer more than necessary when their dog dies. Dr Mary Stewart, a vet teaching at Glasgow Veterinary School, talked to forty owners whose dogs had died. They had all felt some degree of sadness, but twenty-one of them said they had also felt guilty about the death.

Guilt about the death of those close to us – be they human or animal – is common. But with the death of a pet, there is often an extra turn of the screw: we can choose euthanasia for him. In theory it is a great blessing to be able to save our pets from pain and suffering, but in practice the decision about whether or when to take up this option can be agonising. J. R. Ackerley agonised about a lot of things

and he certainly agonised about Queenie's euthanasia, at
the age of sixteen:

> *For three weeks I spoon-fed her with everything, glaxo protein*
> *foods, little bits of raw mince steak, water, milk, putting them*
> *into the pouch of her jaw. She became weaker and thinner. Now*
> *she could not get up at all of her own accord, to walk or to*
> *change position in her bed; I lifted her for everything, and when*
> *she was up she had difficulty in lying down again, slowly,*
> *carefully and awkwardly subsiding as though she had*
> *rheumatism. She got very thin; the bones of her bottom stood*
> *out, her ribs were visible, her stomach sank in. Lying in her bed*
> *under her blanket her eyes were fixed always on me, so loving, so*
> *beautiful. It made the step I had to take in the end all the more*
> *difficult (how I wished she would die, like my aunt, in her sleep),*
> *until she did something that upset me more than her inability to*
> *eat, she began to turn her face to the wall, to turn her back on*
> *me. Then I had her destroyed.*

If you are faced with this decision, the opinion of a vet
whom you trust is invaluable. Although you know your
own dog better than he does, he may be able to help you
decide how much the dog is suffering. More importantly,
he may be able to give you some prognosis and estimate of
the likely effect of treatment. This happened with our first
dog, Mhairi:

> Towards the end of her life, she became very ill with heart
> failure. She was in a miserable state, not able to walk a
> few steps without flopping down and off her food. The
> heart specialist at the Veterinary School, Peter Darke, tried
> combinations of various drugs, without apparent success.
> When she had a fit under the Christmas tree on Christmas
> day, I felt that the time had come for euthanasia. But he
> advised me to hold off, as there was a good chance that
> she would improve if the dosages of the drugs could be
> properly adjusted. And indeed about a week after that she
> did improve. Although she died the following March, her
> final decline was fairly rapid and in the meantime,
> although she was considerably slowed down, she was

able to do most of the things which were important to her. She was able to go to the bottom of the garden and bark at the dog next door. If lifted up the stairs, last thing at night, she was able to carry out what was clearly to her an important duty, to check the little room half-way up the stairs for stray cats. She had once found one there about three years before.

Owners may feel guilty in retrospect about a euthanasia because they feel the decision was based, at least to some extent, on their own feelings and preferences rather than on the medical condition of the dog. For example they may feel that, because of their dread of losing the dog, they delayed euthanasia too long and made him suffer unnecessarily. On the other hand, they may feel guilty that they rid themselves too soon of a dog who was becoming inconvenient and unpleasant to care for: perhaps smelly, incontinent and needing special food. If you do feel guilty about this kind of thing, try not to be too hard on yourself: we are only human and considerations of this kind are bound to influence us. On the other hand, it may save agonising afterwards if, before the euthanasia decision, you can think through the issues and be honest with yourself.

You are more likely to be able to make a reasonable and balanced decision if you have time and if you are able to talk things over as a family. There are some situations, for example if a dog is fatally injured in a road accident and is in great pain, where a decision cannot be postponed; but, in most instances, the euthanasia can wait at least a day. As well as allowing you time to be sure that this is the right decision, it also gives the family time to say goodbye to the dog. Of course, this is very upsetting for everyone at the time, but in the long run it usually feels a much more satisfactory parting.

One of the most painful euthanasia decisions is one which is taken on behavioural grounds – if the dog is liable to bite without warning, for example. One of the reasons why this situation may be so distressing is that the dog himself is not usually suffering, it is the people around him who are suffering. (As I have mentioned in Chapter 4, behaviour problems such as phobias which cause suffering principally to the dog himself can usually be treated and euthanasia is very rarely justified for them.) Also owners are often upset because they feel that the problem is their fault – that they have trained the dog badly for example. But the mistakes which an owner may have made with a dog are almost always reversible. (For advice on how to reverse them, see *Problem Dog*.) It is experiences he may have had as a puppy – not meeting enough people, for example – which leave impressions which are much harder to eradicate. These are usually the breeder's fault. Also a dog's genetic make-up plays a large part in determining his behaviour. So usually owners need not add to their distress by blaming themselves.

In addition to deciding the right time for euthanasia, you will also have to consider where it is to take place and who should be there. You may well feel that your dog would be happier to die at home, rather than at the vet's surgery, especially if he dislikes visits to the vet or if, on this occasion, it promises to be an uncomfortable journey. You may also feel that your dog would be comforted by your presence right up to the end. I have heard some competent and caring vets say that euthanasia is best carried out in the back room of the surgery without the owners present. Their arguments are that the best facilities are available there; that owners may be distressed by the euthanasia, especially if the vet can't find a vein quickly or if the dog gives a reflex gasp as he dies; and that the owner's distress is only upsetting to the dog. This view seems misguided. Its principal aim seems to be to protect the vet from the owner's emotions. Doctors accept that it is appropriate and desirable that a person have his nearest and dearest around him when he dies. Why should the same not apply to a dog? A student may need the privacy of a surgery back room to be able to carry out a euthanasia properly, but an

experienced vet should easily be able to do the job com-
petently at the dog's home, with the owner watching.

So if you want to be with your dog during the euthanasia
or you want it carried out at home, state your wishes
clearly to your vet. If these seem to create a problem for
him, then you should be able to find another vet, in the
same practice, or even in another practice, who will be
willing to carry them out. If your dog does not die in your
presence – whether because you decide it is best that way
or for some other reason – you may still feel you want to see
the body. This may seem an illogical desire – it is not that
you disbelieve the vet who tells you he is dead, for example
– but it is a natural human desire and studies involving
other kinds of deaths shows that it helps the mourning
process. Mothers of still-born babies, for instance, are
much less likely to become stuck later in a state of
unresolved grief if they see their babies' bodies. A sixteen-
year-old girl writes of her German shepherd:

> Tara passed away due to a heart attack. I remember coming home
> and having to get ready to go to the pictures. I also remember
> what I thought was Bess, the springer spaniel, barking, then I
> thought I heard Tara playfully whine back at her. As I was in a
> rush I didn't bother checking on them. When I was at the cinema
> I saw a preview for the film K9 and I remember saying to my
> boyfriend, it looks like Tarbags doesn't it? When I arrived home
> my mum and dad were sat in the front room on the settee. They
> asked me to sit down beside them. Then they began to cry and
> told me they had found Tara dead and had buried her at the top
> of the garden. I remember my heart felt like it was being
> wrenched apart. I had a lump in my throat which wouldn't seem
> to go. I felt my parents had cheated me out of seeing my pal
> Tarbags before she was laid to rest. I ran out the back door to
> where they had buried her and I cried more and said goodbye to
> her. Later I realised why my parents hadn't let me see Tara as
> they told me that her tongue and mouth were blue.

An experienced vet should not be surprised by an owner's
wish to see his dog's body. If he tries to discourage you
without giving an adequate reason (for example that the

body is badly mutilated) then it is he who has a problem with issues of death and loss, not you.

Generally speaking, the death of a human family member has a much greater impact than the death of an animal member. As Mary Stewart puts it, these human bereavements seem 'earth-stopping', in a way which the death of a pet rarely is. On the other hand, there are aspects of a pet's death which can be harder to deal with than that of a person. With a human death there is normally a framework of social conventions and legal requirements to support the bereaved, at least in the early days. There is a general sympathy and understanding for their grief and a funeral service in which they may express it.

When a pet dies, convention does not dictate any particular method of disposing of the body nor any cere-mony to go with it. You can leave your dog for the vet to dispose of, or in some parts of the country there are facilities for cremating pets. Some people seem to find this idea very funny, though I can't see why. Perhaps they have to find it funny because it provides an unsettling reminder of the levelling effect of death: a dog's ashes are not very different from a person's ashes. Since the 'Control of Waste' regulations came into force in 1992, unfortuna-tely it seems that it is illegal to bury your pets in your own garden. When they die, they now become 'clinical waste': apparently you should put the body in a yellow polythene bag marked 'for incineration only' and summon a 'regis-tered contractor' to dispose of it. Because of this legislation, some vets, when a dog dies at their surgery, may try to prevent the owner from taking away the body. This can be countered by telling him that you are aware of the terms of the Act: he may ask you to sign a form absolving him from responsibility.

Religion can provide comfort in a human bereavement, offering the idea that the dead person still exists in a form which is separate from his body; that he is with God and at peace; that the bereaved will eventually be reunited with him. When a dog dies, owners may privately comfort themselves with similar thoughts. But established churches officially don't support these views: they tend to emphasise the uniqueness of human relationships and the human soul. On the other hand, there are individual ministers and priests who take the opposite view and who can offer great comfort.

Unless the dog was a family dog, mourning him can be a lonely process too. Bereaved people find it helpful if those around make allowances for them; they also find it helpful to be able to talk about their feelings, about the death and about the dead person generally. In our society this does not happen as much as it should, even for human bereavements. We like to brush death under the carpet and pretend it does not happen. This is in marked contrast to society's attitude at some times in the past. The Victorians, for example, accepted death. Often they even sentimentalised it. This may have been more helpful to bereaved pet owners – Sir Walter Scott's friends certainly seem to have been very understanding. His son-in-law writes of the death of one of Scott's dogs:

> *He was buried on a fine moonlight night, in the little garden behind the house in Castle Street immediately opposite to the window at which Scott usually sat writing. My wife told me that she remembered the whole family standing in tears about the grave as her father himself smoothed down the turf above Camp, with the saddest expression of face she had ever seen in him. He had been engaged to dine abroad that day, but apologised on account of the death of a dear old friend; and Mr MacDonald Buchanan was not at all surprised that he should have done so, when it came out next morning that Camp was no more.*

Nowadays, with an animal bereavement, the situation tends to be even worse than with a human bereavement. Many people just don't understand what the fuss is about – it's only a dog, after all. Mary Stewart found that 25% of the owners in her study were so distressed by the death of their pet that they could not cope with their normal routine; 8% experienced prolonged grieving with physical symptoms such as loss of appetite. Those who have lived alone with their dog are likely to suffer most. They are often the hardest hit by the loss itself and then they may have no one to talk to about it.

So, without much help from society, an owner often has to manage as best he can when his dog dies. As with the circumstances of the euthanasia, try not to be swept along by the arrangements which others such as the vet may choose to make. If possible, it is a good idea to think out your preferences in advance. Then, if you don't want a post mortem done, say so. If you want to dispose of the body yourself, say so. Burying your dog in a special place or scattering his ashes there can be a great comfort. Also, immediately following the death, you may find it necessary to create some space for yourself, if others do not create it for you. You should give yourself time to grieve: allow yourself to feel sad, angry or whatever else you might feel. Don't force yourself to feel or behave 'normally'. If you find you have to take time out of your work or social life to do this, then don't feel guilty about it. If you feel your employers or friends are unlikely to be understanding, you may have to protect yourself with a few white lies. Try to talk to other people about your feelings. In the United States there are bereavement groups for people whose pets have died. The British tend to be more reticent about formalising subtle human interaction in this way – it seems too crude.

However, I recently received a letter from a Mrs D. G. Parry, reproaching me for a similar comment made in *Problem Dog*:

> It appears that you do not know what has been already achieved in this direction. . . . Being a retired Medical Social Worker I can well understand that people do need help at these times. I have begun training a group of volunteers using my own writings and we now have a counselling service in operation,

known as the Thanet Loss Counselling Service with myself as Director and Chief Counsellor. My telephone number (Thanet 45435) is listed among the Help Lines in one of the local papers. I have personally featured in magazine and newspaper articles and on television and as a result have received enquiries from many parts of Great Britain and one from Washington University.

If you don't find a listening ear among those, such as your family, who 'ought' to understand and you don't feel like contacting a trained counsellor, you may well find help in a less obvious place. The nurse at your veterinary practice may well be receptive: veterinary nurses are more often motivated by love of animals than are vets. Or there may be other people – even some whom you know only slightly – who may be pleased to have you share your experience with them, especially if they also have had a painful animal bereavement. There are a lot of such people around. It is a matter of finding them.

It may also help to put things down on paper. Write about the events and feelings which trouble you most, just as they come to you. Later you might even feel like polishing up what you have written into something which other dog lovers would find helpful. Or you might write a poem: or even paint a picture.

Certainly I found very moving the many accounts I received of the death of dogs and of their owners' experiences at the time and later. It is clear that many people are affected by their dogs' death for a long time afterwards. When he is alive, a dog is usually a constant presence in the house, an intimate part of the owner's daily routine. When he dies, the owner is continually reminded of his absence by little things which now no longer happen or need to be done: no dog to greet you when you come home, no dog to feed at six o'clock, no dog to take for a walk last thing at night. As I mentioned above, owners who live alone with their dogs may find their death harder to cope with because they are alone with their grief. They also tend to be harder hit because the dog often plays a more central part in their domestic routine. People may also be especially affected by their dog's death because it reminds them of other bereavements or stirs up other issues.

I had a very close relationship with my father from the time I was little. I was 24 years old and reasonably mature in that I was a ward sister, when he died. He had been ill with severe angina: frustration made him very short tempered. The bouts of severe depression and bad temper became more frequent, there were times when he felt suicidal. One day after listening to a particular episode of the Archers on the radio (we are talking about 1955) he asked me if I thought psychiatric treatment would help him. Although I have an older sister, for some years my mother and father had turned to me for all manner of advice, just because people treat nurses that way. I knew very little of psychiatry but we had had some lectures during training and I saw no reason why counselling of this kind should not help him to come to terms with his disability. In addition his admission to hospital would give my mother a break and would improve their relationship when he returned. He didn't return. What I did not appreciate was that the local psychiatric hospital was not really the place for a psychiatrically ill man. It was a dreadful place and even now it hurts me to think that was where he spent his last 48 hours. He was not allowed to keep his tablets by his bed and he had a heart attack the second night. I suppose I felt that if I had found out more about the hospital and had advised him not to go, he might not have died. I don't know because I didn't think clearly at that time. I had just found myself a job abroad so that my visits home were curtailed. I think for a long time I played a game of not really believing he was gone.

In September 1979 my old dog Seamus was 14 years old and I had taken in a rescue dog Bruno. He and Seamus became great friends but in December they both became ill. The vet said that there was a new virus called parvo but it was only fatal to very young puppies. Through to the middle of January I used every nursing skill I had ever learnt but it was not enough. The old dog eventually recovered but Bruno died. My distress was out of all proportion. I went to talk to a friend who was a psychologist at the hospital in which I was working and after a few sessions I found I was crying for my father.

We decided to get another puppy. I checked with the vet and with the Department of Veterinary Pathology at Glasgow to find out what to do to protect him. I did everything they said but this was only 1980 and not enough was known at the time. At 4 months of age Derry my Golden Retriever puppy started to vomit in exactly the same way as the others. He had parvo. He survived but at 5 months it was found that he had a myocarditis. As I walked him in the woods one day I told him that I would not let him die. Then I realised the futility of what I said and I suddenly burst into tears of grief that my love and knowledge as a nurse had not been enough to save my father or Bruno. I realised that I was only me. I had not the power of God and having done my best that was all that I could do.

Writing this has not been particularly easy. Derry is now in his eleventh year and still taking his lanoxin. I survived the death of the original dog in 1982 and of my mother last year without any abnormal grief. I have also in a small way been able to help others faced with bereavement distress.

Studies of widows have shown that, paradoxically, those who have had a bad relationship with their husbands may find coming to terms with their bereavement particularly difficult. This is probably because, without being aware of it, they feel very guilty as well as sad. They feel that their angry thoughts about their husbands – maybe at times even murderous thoughts – have magically succeeded in actually killing him. The same happens with dogs. We know that 50% of owners feel guilty about their dogs' deaths and among those who feel particularly guilty are those who have had difficult dogs. If the dog's life ended in euthanasia because of a behavioural problem, then they not only feel as if they were responsible for their dog's death, they know that they actually were responsible. A farmer's wife writes:

As we are in the farming community I feel that we may have a different relationship with our dogs. Because in most cases we have so many stock animals to look after, the dog has two choices: it either fits in and forms a relationship with master and family or it doesn't.

But she also writes:

A crisis I found particularly hard was the decision to have our first dog put to sleep at the age of three. Although he was outwardly healthy, we believe he had an internal problem which made him aggressive in the extreme, both to other dogs and people. When he bit me, the crunch came and I had to make the decision. I could not have had it on my conscience for my scarred arm to be a child's face. Although it does not sound like it, Mufti was greatly loved and we didn't want to lose him. It was the hardest decision I have had to make. I still feel guilty.

Owners have written of strange experiences connected with their dogs' deaths. For example:

My present Honey is a toy apricot poodle. My previous two were miniature apricot poodles. When Honey II died at twelve years I had her cremated as I wanted to be able to keep her remains with me whenever I moved from London. My first Honey had diabetes at eleven and a half years and I used to test her urine each day and give her an insulin injection until she died in my arms at thirteen years four months. She was buried in the garden with a little headstone giving her name and dates and 'In sweet memory and abiding love'. I put an evergreen Pieris 'Flame of the Forest' shrub over her grave and planted lots of 'Angel Tears' daffodils sited next to a dwarf rhododendron 'Temple Belle' with lovely bell-like pink flowers. I put flowers on the grave especially on her anniversaries when I would put a night-light there too. Mostly covered by a flowerpot due to wind and rain but the little light was a symbol of her love in a dark world. Unless I was away from home or ill in bed, I would visit her every day to say I had not forgotten her and to thank her for all the love she gave me. I would feel the stems of the bush and say 'I am through to you Honey' as I felt the roots of the shrub reach down to touch her below.

I did not want to leave Honey behind when I finally moved from London and although the Pieris was a lovely shrub the new owners might want to alter the layout of the garden and I did not want Honey dug up and found by anyone else. I thought that after twelve years there would be some bones in the grave which I could put in a box and take with me when I moved. My mother advised me not to wait till then but to get her up beforehand. I had to wait as I did not want to damage the flowers or new leaves on the shrub and living on clay soil it was either as hard as concrete or sticky. Also one has to be in the right frame of mind to open a grave. However one Sunday more than thirteen years after Honey's death I moved the shrub with a lot of soil around the roots and then I put my spade under the plastic bundle. I knew by the weight she was still there and so she was – just as I had last seen her. I had wrapped her in one of my cardigans which I had knitted (every stich a kiss for her) then one of my dresses and finally a sheet of flowered plastic. She was just as I had buried her with her two favourite toys, the only thing missing were the roses I put with her: they had gone without a trace.

I was in a quandary: did I rebury her and then dig her up again when I moved? As I did not want to leave her behind I decided to have her cremated too. So now I have the ashes of both Honey I and Honey II with me. Now, to me, my Honey I performed a miracle in waiting for me after death. Lots of murder victims are found unrecognisable or just skeletons left – not my Honey, she stayed with me after death, so you can see how important she is to me in my life.

I would rather be buried with my Honeys in a pet cemetery but that would not be allowed and they do not allow pets in human cemeteries, so I have left instructions for certain items to be buried with me, a couple of which contain the ashes of my Honeys, so we shall be together always – I hope.

More common is the experience of seeing the dead dog. Mostly, these sightings are comforting, at any rate not alarming; for example, an unmarried woman in her sixties writes of her Springer spaniel who died three years earlier at the age of twelve:

Up to the earlier part of this year (not so much now) I used to see him quite a lot. Usually, when washing up, he would come in from outside in the hope that there might be the odd snack about for him.

This kind of experience is reported perhaps even more often by relatives after a human bereavement. They often have a strong feeling of the dead person's presence. Sometimes they see or hear him. So different is this experience from anything which has happened to them before, that people often feel that they are going mad. But whatever the psychological explanation for them, it is clear that these experiences are so common that they should be regarded as normal.

Sometimes these re-visits are unpleasant, usually when the dog in life has been problematic:

> *On my eleventh birthday I was given a five week old Labrador cross. I named him Rory. He was my dog and I loved him very, very much. He was highly strung and could be aggressive and not very well trained (as it was left up to me). I used to tell him all my teenage problems etc. Well, when I was fourteen, going on fifteen, Rory bit my sister badly and my vet recommended he should be put to sleep. I took him along with my mum. It broke my heart, to this day I will never forget him and still have old photographs. About one year after his death I was upstairs in my house. I wasn't even thinking of Rory when I heard a thump of the living-room door downstairs. I could hear Rory scraping at the carpet and howling. I knew he wanted to come to me, he used to always do this, my heart was in my mouth. I was very frightened. I ran out of the house. I have always wondered if I should have entered the room. This was not my imagination. This was definitely Rory.*

Occasionally, it is someone else, not the owner, who sees the dog:

> *I had a standard poodle, pure white and beautiful, he was a proper rascal, he stayed with me for eleven years. We were inseparable and how we loved each other, he loved all his family, house and garden, he took us all over and that was his life. He died in my arms at the Veterinary School. How I miss him, it hurts very badly not to see him: that of course is unreasonable, I know. Mostly I laugh when I think about him. The only noteworthy mention is – a little girl and her mother stopped on the pavement and said, 'What a nice dog was sitting at the window.' He always waited there for me coming back from the shops. I looked around when I got in, I didn't see him. Who knows, perhaps he guards the house when I am out! By the way, he hated children, he couldn't stand the sight of them!*

Even more occasionally, someone makes a hobby of it:

I have been involved with spiritualism for about eighteen years, at first I was very sceptical and treated it all as a joke. I learned quite quickly that I had mediumistic ability. My son, who is a perfectly normal rugby-playing young man, also has this gift.

Over the years of my son and daughter growing up we had two dogs and a cat. All lived a long time. The cat passed first and there was one point in time when my husband (who is not psychic) and myself clearly heard a 'meeow' in the kitchen when we opened the fridge door. The oldest dog passed at seventeen years old and was often seen by other mediums coming to the house, but not by me. I used to see a hazy figure at night by the bed where he slept but it was never clear and I put it down to wishful thinking.

In 1983 we started to become involved with showing and breeding G. S. D.s and my daughter became a veterinary nurse, so we began to have much more contact with animals, mainly dogs. An elderly aunt was taken into hospital and we took her eighteen year old Jack Russell bitch. The animal had been neglected and was in need of veterinary treatment. She was actually a bit of a nuisance but she enjoyed living with all our dogs. She only lived two months with us but for that time she was well cared for. When she was put to sleep it was because of a stroke, not because she was unwanted. She came through to my son when he was talking to a friend who is also a medium, and later on I was told she was in the room with me. We hadn't particularly loved this dog but had given her compassionate care when she needed it.

Bessie was a fifteen month old G.S.D. that had an epileptic fit, her owner was terrified and shut her in the garden. My daughter's employer asked me to look after her for a few days and observe her behaviour and await rehoming. G.S.D. welfare would not take her because of the Fit and she must be put to sleep. We were very sad for her and made a lot of fuss of her while she was with us. Six months later when talking to a friend on the phone, she suddenly said, 'I have got a dog here with you, it is called Bess and it lived with you for three days, it was very happy with you.' This particular medium hadn't had a lot to do with animals and she was really surprised, so was I because the dog had been with us for such a short time. Again, we hadn't formed a deep link with the animal but we had given it compassion and care.

The dogs I have owned and loved for a very long time are able

*to project an image that I can see, the one that died young,
although I loved her very much, doesn't seem able to do that. I
would love to see her as I do the others. When other people have
come to me for readings, all sorts of domestic animals and birds
come through, they appear as pictures in the mind quite clearly
and often their name into the mind as well. Sometimes they can
be seen moving around the person they have come to visit.*

*Our latest rescue is a tiny G.S.D. bitch, she is very fit and
well but is showing signs of being psychic herself. My husband is
shortly retiring and we are hoping to have a small kennels and a
little sanctuary where I shall be able to observe animals that are
rescued before and after they have passed.*

A question which usually arises after the death of a dog is
whether to replace him. Some owners do this automatically. Others are more reluctant: they may feel unwilling to
start again the same sequence of becoming attached to a
dog, only to be bereaved again. They may simply feel too
sad and depressed to take on a new set of responsibilities.
Mary Stewart found that all of her bereaved owners who
got a new dog were glad that they had done so. All of those
who experienced prolonged grief were reluctant to replace
their dog, but when they did were greatly helped.

While no other dog can fully replace the one who came
before him, there are some aspects of his relationship with
you which can be replaced: his constant companionship,
for example, his dependence on you, his need of walks.
But some owners have unrealistic expectations of their
dog's successor. I often see problem dogs whose owners
complain how different he is from their previous dog of the
same breed: perhaps he is less affectionate, less obedient or
less tolerant of separation. I sometimes wonder how
perfect these dead dogs really were, whether, perhaps,
they have become sanctified by death and that, in their
day, they too did annoying things which their owners have
forgotten about.

There is probably a right and a wrong time to get a new
dog. Just after the death of the old one may be too soon. At
that time you may be tempted to take the first dog who

presents himself, merely to fill the gap; or you may, without realising it, try to get a dog who is an exact replica of the one who has just died. This can give rise to the kind of problems described. If you give yourself time for reflection, you might decide for example that this time you want a bitch rather than a dog, or that you would be better with a dog of a different breed.

Finally, here are John Galsworthy's views on canine mortality:

> *Do they know, as we do, that their time must come? Yes, they know, at rare moments. No other way can I interpret those pauses of his latter life, when, propped on his forefeet, he would sit for long minutes quite motionless – his head drooped, utterly withdrawn; then turn those eyes of his and look at me. That look said more plainly than all words could: 'Yes, I know that I must go!' If we have spirits that persist – they have. If we know after our departure who we were – they do. No one, I think, who really longs for truth, can ever glibly say which it will be for dog or man – persistence or extinction of our consciousness. There is but one thing certain – the childishness of fretting over that eternal question. Whichever it be, it must be right, the only possible thing. He felt that too, I know; but then, like his master, he was what is called a pessimist.*
>
> *My companion tells me that, since he left us, he has once come back. It was Old Year's Night, and she was sad, when he came to her in visible shape of his black body, passing round the dining-room from the window-end, to his proper place beneath the table at her feet. She saw him quite clearly; she heard the padding tap-tap of his paws and very toe-nails; she felt his warmth brushing hard against the front of her skirt. She thought then that he would settle down upon her feet, but something disturbed him, and he stood pausing, pressed against her, then moved out toward where I generally sit, but was not sitting that night. She saw him stand there, as if considering; then at some sound or laugh, she became self-conscious, and slowly, very slowly, he was no longer there. Had he some message, some counsel to give, something he would say, that last night of the last year of all he had watched over us? Will he come back again?*
>
> *No stone stands over where he lies. It is on our hearts that his life is engraved.*

13 ● *Dogs and the Supernatural*

'M. R-W', *Dog World*, March 1991:

During the War, I used to walk down to see a friend who lived some four miles away from Mansergh, passing the back gates of a mansion. One fine summer's evening in broad daylight, I had an Irish setter with me. As we passed the gates on the way home, she suddenly became absolutely terrified, trying to escape and trembling with fear and staring at one of the gate-posts. I pulled her past it and on down the long straight road, but she walked backwards, staring back, pulling and growling and trembling and barking.

Some form of thought transmittance took place and I suddenly knew what she was seeing, and that was a dirty, shabby-looking man, dressed in tattered brown Cavalier's dress and a floppy Cavalier-dated hat, as unlike the laughing Cavalier as could be, but of that exact date by his dress. He had a horrid leer on his face and watched us walk down the road till we turned the bend. I knew him as well as if I had seen him and thought he was a demobbed soldier, fallen on bad times and indeed a bad, rough sort of man. I must say that frightened me and I never went home that way again.

I mentioned this to someone on the estate and they said indeed I had got it right, because a deserter from the Cavalier army had murdered a servant-girl and that was their trysting place. I can tell you that shook me, but an even more curious event was to follow. The Oxenholme stag-hounds met by that gate and in the middle of a very busy meet with hounds, horses, foot-followers and all, bustling about, my psychic cousin came up to me and said, 'There is something simply horrid standing by the gate-post, I don't know what it is but it is a man and he is BAD.' She could not stand it so went home. Now neither she nor I saw that ghost but the Irish setter did.

My other experience was that we had a haunted bookcase-cum-

writing-desk to which we knew a ghost walked. He used to come through the corner of the sitting-room and any dog in the house used to half get up to welcome him, thumping his tail, and then look puzzled and obviously did not understand what he was seeing. Some were slightly frightened but most just didn't understand, but thought he was a sort of half-welcome stranger. Then the desk used to creak loudly as though someone were opening the cupboards. After a bit the dogs would subside again. We knew they were seeing someone, and then one night I saw him and after that I saw him several times. So I KNOW that they can see ghosts. I saw him myself. Who he was I do not know, though I tried to find out. But when we moved, I sold that bit of furniture without a pedigree and hoped the buyers were not psychic or they did not have a house-dog.

Dogs often feature in accounts of the paranormal. Sometimes they have a reassuring function. In the example just given, the Irish setter is a parental dog with special powers to spy out bad people even when they are invisible. The dead dogs in Chapter 12, who reappeared to their owners as ghosts (or whose mortal remains are miraculously preserved, as in the case of Honey) were for the most part comforting. Such stories are comforting to other dog owners, too. One of our chief dreads is separation from those we love; the most irrevocable separation is death. These stories are comforting because they deny the finality of this separation, rather like that passage so often read out at memorial services: 'Death is nothing at all. I have only slipped into the next room . . .'

If, on the other hand, a dog embodies emotions which it finds disturbing and which you want to be rid of, a dog-ghost can be frightening. Examples of this are the 'Hounds of Hell' in Chapter 9 which crop up in various countries and cultures presaging death; and the girl in Chapter 12 whose epileptic and savage dog came back to haunt her.

Dogs appear often in stories of the supernatural partly because, as we have seen throughout this book, they provoke and embody strong primitive feelings. But another reason is that at times they do seem to possess supernatural powers or powers of extra-sensory perception. There are plenty of stories of dogs behaving strangely before earthquakes or refusing to cross bridges which, minutes later, collapse. The explanation of this kind of thing probably lies in the fact that some of a dog's senses are keener than ours, that they detect sounds or vibrations which are imperceptible to us. Similarly, a dog's expertise in reading body language probably explains many of the accounts of telepathy between dogs and owners, such as the owner of Livingstone in Chapter 6, who knew when she was going to take a bath.

A story of the supernatural needs to be skilfully written for it to be frightening, moving or unsettling. It is all too easy for it to become ridiculous or even boring. One feature which tends to dull a story's edge is repetition. Most of us feel that a paranormal world, to be plausible even in fiction, must be accessible to us only rarely and surprisingly. If the paranormal becomes an everyday occurrence, then we find it so implausible that we lose interest or find it funny. This is partly why M. R-W's first ghost story about the Irish setter and the Cavalier is so much more telling than the second one about the haunted bookcase. It is also why we are more moved by accounts (like that of Galsworthy) of owners who are visited by their dead dogs once or twice than by the medium's account of all the dead dogs she has been in touch with.

True stories of the paranormal need, for maximum impact, another ingredient. They need some kind of external validation of the experience. M. R-W's Cavalier story has that ingredient: *after* the dog has seen the ghost, M. R-W learns that a Cavalier soldier murdered a servant girl there. Her bookcase story does not have that validation: it needs, for example, the new owner of the house to get in touch with her to complain about the bookcase's effect on her budgies.

This brings us to the question of whether dogs do indeed possess paranormal powers. The problem of what is going on when people or dogs see ghosts is too complex to examine here, but the question of whether dogs have extra-sensory perception is more easily tackled. As we have seen, many accounts of so-called ESP can be easily explained in terms of a dog's superior but normal abilities. Sometimes it is more difficult. For example, consider this account, written by one owner who answered my questionnaire, a married woman in her seventies:

> *My second dog, a Jack Russell-type mongrel bitch, adored my husband. He often worked late. When he was not working late, she always went and lay down on the front door mat at the time he would be leaving the office. On the days he was working late she didn't do so, although the days he worked late differed from week to week. One day when he was supposed to be working late, I took her for her evening stroll at his normal, early home-coming time. She didn't want to go, so I put her on the lead and when we reached the grass, I released her and walked on. She didn't run ahead and I turned to see her slinking back to the house. Just as I reached the house myself I saw her rapturously greeting my husband on the doorstep.*

Scientific method demands that we try to explain peculiar happenings in terms of physical laws we already know about. If we try to explain the above account in this way, we must suppose that the Jack Russell was able to distinguish between her master's normal and late working days by noticing differences in his body language when he left for work in the morning. Most dogs are capable of adjusting their expectations of the day according to their observations of their owners' behaviour in the morning: this is how they tell weekends and holidays from weekdays. Alternatively, she might have noticed differences in her mistress's body language in the evening, when her master was or was not due to come home. In either case, one would have to suppose in addition that, on the day when he came back unexpectedly early, when he left in the morning there was some uncertainty in his mind as to whether he would need to work late or not. Although he told his wife he would be working late, he could have conveyed this uncertainty in his tone of voice or behaviour, an uncertainty which could have been noticed by the dog or by his wife.

As long as an explanation, however complicated, of this kind of incident is available in terms of natural forces, it must be preferred to one which invokes telepathy. Another trouble with anecdotal evidence of this kind is that because it deals with unpredicted events cropping up unexpectedly in the course of people's lives, all the different possible explanations of them cannot be tested. What scientists investigating all kinds of paranormal phenomena quite rightly demand is examples of telepathy, ESP, or whatever, occurring under controlled, laboratory conditions. Unfortunately, this usually turns out to be difficult to arrange. Most people have a telepathic experience at some time in their lives. It usually happens between people who have a close relationship and at a time of heightened emotion – for example, when one of the pair is very ill or very upset. This means it is very difficult to study telepathy under experimental conditions.

As far as I know, no one has yet attempted a scientific study of dog telepathy. But it seems to me that, to the owner, the experience of dog–owner telepathy is as real as the experiences of person–person telepathy. It is also just as plausible. The main difference between a dog brain and a human brain is that the cortex, which is needed for rational thinking, is much smaller in a dog. The parts of a dog's brain which are responsible for the experiences of emotion are as well developed as the same parts of a human brain.

I would be most interested to hear from any owners who think they may have telepathic dogs or dogs who see ghosts (or, for that matter, owners who have seen ghost-dogs).

Part V
Conclusion

14 ● *What Should We Feel about Dogs?*

Dog owners love to listen to advice. As well as the training manuals mentioned in Chapter 7, public library shelves are crammed with much-borrowed books on how to show your dog, groom her, breed from her, feed her or treat her ailments. With some honourable exceptions, most of these books consist of a string of imperatives, without any rationale to back up their recommendations. In the same way I find that some owners who consult me about their problem dogs have already tried out an amazing range of remedies: herbal pills, homeopathy, rape alarms, choke chains, rolled-up newspapers, spaying, tranquillisers, taking the dog for long walks, excluding the dog from the bedroom, feeding the dog after the family. This is partly a measure of the owner's desperation, but what impresses me is that many have no idea of how the method they are trying is supposed to work.

Others enjoy listening to dog advice, not with the aim of following it, but in order to agree or disagree with it. The dog papers regularly carry articles by vets on, for example, the life-cycle of the dog flea or the genetics of hip dysplasia, but the regular columnists and correspondence columns ignore this scientific material. They fire polemics back and forth at each other, blasting off with imperative and counter-imperative.

Towards the beginning of my career as a dog behaviourist, I taught an evening class in dog psychology for a term at the extra-mural department of Edinburgh University. I never repeated the performance. Although the class was over-subscribed, and the room filled to overflowing, very few in the audience were interested in what I had to say. My lectures were called things like 'How a dog thinks' or 'Social behaviour in the wolf pack'. The ordinary dog owners, who made up about a third of my audience, were not interested in acquiring this general knowledge. They wanted to know how to make Rover come when they called or stop Bramble lifting his leg on the laundry basket. The third of the audience which consisted of breeders and trainers were not much taken with these topics either. They were interested in handing out advice to the ordinary owners or, even better, in disagreeing with any recommendations which I might be lured into making. The remaining third of the audience consisted of retired Edinburgh worthies who had paid a lump sum to become 'Friends of the Extra-Mural Department'. This entitled them to attend any course without extra charge. Most of them snoozed or chatted gently to one another.

Of course, even the most avid consumer of advice can follow only a fraction of it. Much of it comes in the form of prohibitions. If owners tried to follow all of even the most common ones, they and their dogs would lead bleak and restricted lives. They would never allow their dogs to jump up on them, bark at the postman, chew things, sit on the furniture, beg for tit-bits at meals, sleep on the beds or go in the kitchen. They would never touch their dogs without washing their hands afterwards (does anyone take any notice of this one?). Above all, they would never forget that their dogs were only dogs.

I am uneasily conscious that this book contains even more prohibitions which, taken out of context, could further dampen and deaden an owner's pleasure. The primary purpose of this book is to provoke thought and insight, not to prevent owners from treating their dogs as children or parents or from taking pleasure in rescuing and nursing them or from keeping housefuls of them. But if people enjoy their dogs in these ways with some degree of awareness of what they are doing, then they may be able to make their lives and their dogs' lives happier.

Certainly owners should remember that their dogs are dogs, but this should add pleasure to the relationship, rather than placing restrictions on it. According to psychoanalysts, one of the hallmarks of a mature relationship is that the partner is treated as a separate individual with his own ideas, preoccupations and needs. He is not seen merely as an extension of oneself or felt to exist solely for the purpose of gratifying one's own needs. He plays a key role in one's internal drama, but he plays it as himself. In the same way, an owner can love a dog passionately and in any of the ways described in this book and, at the same time, allow him to be a dog. For example, it could be said that Queenie was the love of J. R. Ackerley's life, but he never forgot she was a dog. In fact, one of his chief delights was observing and trying to make sense of her behaviour.

Nowadays, this kind of attitude is increasingly common. It is one of the ways in which Western society has unquestionably made progress over the last fifty years. Human and animal rights may still be abused on a massive scale, the number of jobless or homeless people may be on the increase, pigs and hens may be factory-farmed, but there is a growing awareness that even if the feelings and needs of a person or animal are different from ours, those feelings and needs are real and valid. We have come a long way since Descartes and his clockwork dogs.

Bibliography

(*denotes recommended for further reading)

*Ackerley, J. R., *My Dog Tulip* (Penguin, London, 1989)
*Anderson, R. K., Hart, B. L. and Hart, L. A., *The Pet
Connection* (Center to Study Human–Animal
Relationships and Environments, Minneapolis, 1984)
Adorno, T. W., Fenkel-Brunswick, E., Levinson, D. J.
and Sandford, R. N., *The Authoritarian Personality*
(Harper, New York, 1950)
*Bannister, D. and Fransella, F. *Inquiring Man: the
Psychology of Personal Constructs* (Routledge, London,
1986)
*Beck, A. and Katcher, A., *Between Pets and People* (C.P.
Putnam, New York, 1983)
Berryman, J. C., Howells, K. and Lloyd-Evans, M., 'Pet
Owner Attitudes to Pets and People', *Veterinary Record*,
117 (1985), pp. 659–61
Briggs, Jean, *Never in Anger* (Harvard University Press,
Cambridge Mass., 1970)
*Dale-Green, Patricia, *Dog* (Rupert Hart-Davis, London,
1966)
De Viney, E., Dickert, J. and Lockwood, R., 'The Care of
Pets Within Child Abusing Families', *International
Journal for the Study of Animal Problems*, 4 (1983), pp.
321–9
Felthous, A. R., 'Aggression Against Cats, Dogs and
People', *Child Psychiatry and Human Development*, 10
(1980), pp. 169–77
*Fogle, B. (ed.), *Interrelations between People and Pets*
(Charles C. Thomas, Springfield, Ill., 1981)

*Haddon, Celia, *Faithful to the End: the Daily Telegraph Anthology of Dogs* (Headline Book Publishing, London, 1991)

Hirsh-Pasek, K. and Treiman, R., 'Doggerel: Motherese in a New Context', *Journal of Child Language*, 9 (1982), pp. 229–37

*Katcher, A. H. and Beck, A. M. (eds), *New Perspectives on our lives with Companion Animals* (Pennsylvania University Press, Philadelphia, 1983)

Kelly, G., *Psychology of Personal Constructs* (W. W. Norton, New York, 1955)

Klinghammmer, E. (ed.), *The Behaviour and Ecology of Wolves* (Garland Press, New York, 1979)

Kellert, S. R. and Felthous, A. R., 'Childhood Cruelty toward Animals among Criminals and Non-Criminals', Proceedings of the International Symposium on Human–Pet Relationships, Austrian Academy of Sciences, 1985

Kinsey, A. C., Pomeroy, W. B. and Martin, C. E., *Sexual Behaviour in the Human Male* (W. B. Saunders, Philadelphia, 1948)

Kinsey, A. C., Pomeroy, W. B., Martin, C. E. and Gebhard, P. H., *Sexual Behaviour in the Human Female* (W. B. Saunders, Philadelphia, 1953)

Lorenz, Konrad Z., *King Solomon's Ring* (Methuen, London, 1952)

*Merlen, R. H. A., *De Canibus: Dog and Hound in Antiquity* (J. A. Allen, London, 1971)

Most, Konrad, *Training Dogs: A Manual* (Popular Dogs, London, 1951)

*O'Farrell, Valerie, *Problem Dog: Behaviour and Misbehaviour*, revised edition (Methuen, London, 1992)

*Parker, Peter, *Ackerley: A Life of J. R. Ackerley* (Constable, London, 1989)

Pollard, John, *Wolves and Werewolves* (Robert Hale, London, 1964)

*Ritvo, Harriet, *The Animal Estate: the English and Other*

Creatures in the Victorian Age (Harvard University Press, Cambridge, Mass., 1987)

Roth, B., 'Never Give your Heart to a Dog to Tear – a Contribution to the Study of Animal–Human Bonding' (unpublished manuscript)

Roslin-Williams, Anne, *The Border Terrier* (Witherby, London, 1983)

*Serpell, J., *In the Company of Animals* (Basil Blackwell, Oxford, 1986)

*Serpell, J., (ed.) (in press), *The Domestic Dog* (Cambridge University Press, Cambridge)

Shewell, P. C. and Nancarrow J. D., 'Dogs that Bite', *British Medical Journal*, 303 (1991), pp. 1512–14

Stewart M., 'Comparative Bereavement', Newsletter of the Group for the Study of the Human–Companion Animal Bond, 2 (1981), pp 4–12

Watt, S., *Companion Animal Cruelty* (unpublished MSc thesis, University of Edinburgh, 1991)

Wigan, Felicity, *The English Dog at Home* (Chatto and Windus, London, 1986)

Woodhouse, Barbara, *Dog Training My Way* (Barbara Woodhouse, Rickmansworth, 1973)

Index